Alkebulan

Volume 1: Foundations

By

Dawei

B180 Basketball, Inc.
P.O. Box 2406
Midland, MI 48641-2406
www.b180basketball.com

Published by B180 Basketball, Inc. 2-16-24

ISBN: (hc) 979-8-9913306-1-9
ISBN: (sc) 979-8-9913306-2-6
ISBN: (e) 979-8-218-37759-5

Library of Congress Control Number:

2024916761

Contents

Theory of Self-Actualization

All things in the world and the human as a living being has followed a basic needs approach to life and happiness. Since the beginning of time humans have had dominion over all things living in the world. A crossroads develops within the soul of the human as changes occur. Challenges related to mental health, happiness, and purpose develops in all beings. The human living as a being in the world must seek self-actualization along with basic needs at the beginning of life in order to find and deliver everlasting truth. The human must find out its origin.

The human must find out what it can do as a human living on earth.

The human must find out what it wants to do as a human living on earth.

The human must find out what it wants to give to the world with love.

The human must find out what it is planning to give with love to the world unconditionally.

The World:
Beginning of Time

Self-Actualization

Less Time

The World:
Present Day

Self-Actualization

More Time

Crossroads

Basic Needs Only

Self Actualization and Basic Needs

Description:

The world has followed the basic needs approach to life and happiness. A crossroads developed as the world continuously changed.   Increased challenges related to mental health, happiness, and purpose developed. The world now must seek self-actualization and basic needs at the beginning of life. This is needed for the evolution of mankind.

Complete basic needs and find out who you are, what you can do, what do you want to do, what you want to give to the world, and how you will do it.

Caste Systems

The caste system developed during the early years when the world first formed. Adam had fallen and the spirit of God had left man.

The people of that time began to rule themselves and place order and control over the people based on various features that they saw in the world.

All of the people during that time before Jesus communicated with God by God's presence, a man of God, or through a prophet. The holy ghost did not live within man because the spirit of man was dead. This was because man sinned. When Adam sinned, that made all humans be born with sin.

When Jesus was born, he was born through a woman by the holy ghost. Jesus was born without sin. Jesus had the full and complete power of the holy ghost within him.

This caused the people that created the caste systems to continuously try to develop ways to limit the individuals that were restored by the giving of the holy ghost back to man through and from Jesus Christ, The Son of Man and The Son of God.

Your gift to the world is what you see as a solution to the problems in the world. It bothers you because others don't see it.

Happiness is harnessed and received by the individual that is

wholeheartedly true to God, their gift, and to their neighbor.

Awareness

Happenings

As the world constantly changes, what happens to you, what's happening in the world, and what you want to make happen in the future will be molded by the love that you give to your neighbor. It doesn't matter what background or ethnic group the individual comes from. It doesn't matter if the individual is friendly to you in return. What matters is the change that you decide to make happen for yourself and the person. Make the change that's filled with the complete awareness of God's love for all beings.

Emotions

Emotions steer the soul. Salvation can be attained if the emotions that are nurtured are those that create a better future for all of mankind. Disciplining the emotions of the heart enables a person to learn how to become a spiritual being that has a body that is controlled for all that is good. Caress the pain and hurt that's felt from worldly happenings with the vision and faith of what's to come. Those that fall down to their knees and plead for the end of the pain while asking "why me?" is something that's done daily. If only they understood that what was ultimately created could be the solution to another's prayer and the beginning of inner peace.

Finding God

To find God a person must bless his neighbor with his whole heart and seek himself. The belief of inner peace is found at the mouth of the river. The river flows with love and leads to unconditional love without measure. To touch the heart of a stranger, the person that reaches out gives love from the past like new.

Clear Mind Focus

The magic of getting what you want begins with focus. The ultimate dream, goal, wish, or accomplishment is shared with the lord every step upon the journey. The continuous vision and thought of achievement begins to create a reality as it is seen.

Open the door to a better world by bringing the dreams of the heart to the doorsteps of God's will. The hurt and pain that accompanies the vision is the journey completed that fulfills a just life.

A clear mind focus must be established to know, believe,

and understand your dream and what it is that you need to do to make that dream come true.

<u>Letting Go</u>

To give your all and live life to find out that it's more that you must give requires a new vision. A person must let go of the way the world was viewed in the past and use it as fuel to build a new life that makes the world better.

Only you can witness what has happened or what will happen to you in flesh. Life is mended by the continuous reach and connection to God.

To let go means to dismantle the love of your most prized possessions and give them away in order to walk in God. A new world depends on your decision to let go.

The dreams and memories will seem to never leave your thoughts. Grab hold to the everlasting words of the lord and set yourself free with a new beginning. The love that's found is refreshing and as beautiful as a dove's wings in mid-flight. That secret place where you and God meet must be as strong as the glare of the stars in the still of the night.

Death & Dying

When a loved one leaves this world the hurt and pain never seems to end. Laying your head on the softest pillow doesn't heal the wounds of the good times that remind you of the person.

Death and dying has a way of building a person's inner core. Knowing that the energy of death will ultimately be witnessed by all; lasting life can be discovered by delivering love and happiness even in death.

A new journey begins upon death. The being exists in a familiar form to those who seek. To control death a person must be fed from the mouth of the lord. Then and only then can deliverance of the promise be fulfilled with all that is true. Find the only love that is true and continuously drink from it's bottomless ocean to beat death and dying.

Imagination

The imagination of man creates reality. The burning belief that it will happen even though it will hurt encourages those who seek. Never seen, heard, touched, thought, or suggested is what is trapped within every being. The disregard of not knowing the full outcome intrigues the passionate souls. Even in failure imagination runs wild. It knows that the unseen will eventually be

seen. Imagination harnesses the passion and love deep within the

hearts of man. Imagination connects the heart of man with the will

of God and creates tomorrow.

Giving

Give with love from God

What you see, hear, feel, touch, smell, eat, read, believe, and all that is consumed is what you become. The more you consume of something is what you will produce and become. In order to give love to the world, you must become a divine all loving and forgiving being, creator, and give the bread of life as the lord. To use the instruments and elements of the world to give from the heart is done to organize that what is within. Defeat temptations. What is given must be pure with unconditional love.

The lord makes it possible for God to give love to you with full authority. Capture the moments alone. Take what is given and understand your true mission. Created to create love. That's what is deep within the eyes of the ones that see it fully completed. Give your full love with all of your blessings even in defeat. Love thy neighbor was spoken. Therefore, you will never be alone. Every dream must be completed with a sealed love blessing and eternal growth that will never be broken.

Understanding the Cause

When man is weak, and he still gives his all it's God's will that was ultimately given in order for man to create tomorrow. Deceit and hate has temporarily damaged the soul of mankind. Greed and worldly possessions are defeated as man grows in the lord.

A man can't be man without spirit. A just spirit molds man into a being that gives unconditional love as God. The wrong that you see in the world is what it is that you must make correct and defeat. Even at your worst you are the best because you are walking with God to defeat the cause.

A New World

Love flows purely from heart to heart, soul to soul, and all that is seen to the unseen. You give life to a new love that is pure. The love resembles the love that you were given through your own darkest moments. You were given blessings and vowed to forget.

To share what only you can share with the new world that's created, look past all that is seen and seek the beginnings of truth. That is where the beginning, end, and creation waits for time and connection.

Connecting

Make God your closest friend. Trust and show love through all your experiences in life. A close friend believes. A close friend knows that what seems to be a close friendship there is more that is unseen.

Even during a doubt of presence or desertion when things go bad, what is stored inside of man is caressed, nurtured, trusted, and guided beyond death. The stronger the belief, the stronger the gift is nurtured. When man leaves God, God doesn't leave man. Growth occurs and the ultimate connection is shown inside the beauty that enters the world and gives timeless unconditional love to generations.

Taking Action

Understanding the ultimate reason why you are doing what you are doing by giving must be accomplished. Loud and clear the hurt and pain of those that suffer is seen and felt. The strength of your belief of what you have to give and of that from those that suffer carries the gift through each stage.

The weakness that is felt becomes temporary as the individual begins to see what is not seen. Action involves walking in a new light that develops the ultimate gift that you give to those that are unborn.

Discrete

Give love that is unseen. Give happiness to another so that it is unseen. Provide water when no water is seen. Run to the lord and take what is given to you and build the new you. Special is what you are carrying inside of you. Discrete love is what has been given to you now and even before birth. Listen to the cries of your neighbor and silence them with a touch of the hand that developed and healed your own pains.

Entering without a scent carries weight. Leaving love for tomorrow causes life to make a change for all that is good.

Your Best

Crying and overcoming the hurt of what has become leads a person on a new journey. A heart was given with all that it had. The passing of the correct gift leaves the lord glad.

Year by year there were dreams of the ultimate ending only to realize that what was nurtured needed God's hand. Look beyond self-doubt. Understand that the strength of spirit and man unites to deliver love to each neighbor just as it was planned.

Giving your best is a purpose driven with passion, heart, and love. Unwavering faith of what is seen in the unseen is what keeps man alive. Failure after failure and cry after cry, the tears that's shed builds tomorrow. Give your best and know that it is finished and nurtured to heal another's sorrow.

Change

The Journey's Mission

You see the mission complete before it starts. The journey day by day, month by month, and year by year doesn't defeat you. The everlasting love and gift that you are sharing shines brightly. True love is hard to find, and you've found it.

You've given your best during each step of the mission while looking towards another day to defeat the challenges that cross your path. It seems like you know exactly what to do to bring the gift forward even during times of despair. A wish, a prayer, and a since of everlasting connection lets you know that God is there.

The journey's mission is an answered prayer that helps you find you. The inner voice guides the happiness that is seen and given despite the misery.

Change builds the help that man seeks.

Change creates and makes man weak.

Change uncovers man and truth.

Change opens man to youth.

Change nurtures love.

Change is heaven sent from the living God above.

The Unknown

Build and let go. The person that develops within will be worth the journey. Know that the pain of the path taken is not a choice. The beauty of it is that a person can prepare the unknown for the unknown by giving their heart unconditionally. Wherever man goes, whatever man does, togetherness within the soul of man clears the path for what's to come. Trust and faith meets ambition and truth brings forth the unknown.

The change for all that is good prepares a just soul for the wrath of what is seen by the naked eye. Surely, I tell you that man will grow while striving to reach the lord and letting out a familiar cry.

The unknown seeks truth to bring it to light. The fear that's felt is overcome by the love that's given to a vision at first sight.

Life Saver

Entering unexpectedly, the gift that's received rebuilds man. Discard the past for a foundation that's pure. A person is rescued from within. The new love shines in everything that they do, everywhere they go, and in every person that they give love to.

To make a change, a person must run pass what is seen and be determined to save his neighbor with love. Despite the background or makeup, the neighbor waits patiently for the love from the life saver. The neighbor needs the true love that's given because it touches eternity. The neighbor accepts the love, grows, believes, and then gives.

Inner Strength

Look past the self. Eliminate all worldly happenings, possessions, and thoughts. Enter the unknown where there is that which begins and ends. The source of all that is good awaits the man that seeks.

Love, happiness, and all that is true is connected to the source that creates all. For it to be given with love as it was created, man must become truth.

As man grows, the thoughts of the past, present, future, and the unknown becomes understood. This in turn builds inner strength in the spirit of man.

Forgiving

A slave of a slave of a slave looks for truth. A peasant seeks salvation only to find that it's unlimited in all that is true. All that is created in that which is seen is ultimately judged in the unseen. The seed of life is given with unconditional love. Water flows constantly through man and gives life. Man was nurtured in love before the release to all that is seen by the normal eye. The decision to choose what is true in the world is what makes man to surely die. Forgiveness of sin was blessed by God. A gift was given in return to deliver man to man. If man becomes one, forgiveness is shown in the just gifts delivered to man.

Walking Away

As the tears escape the love that's deep inside, the hurt that's felt blinds the simple man and worldly pride. Eliminating the self and seeking truth in times of loneliness and pain opens a state of unknown and freedom without action.

As the love from God pours into a being, there remains an empty self that needs to be released. The understanding of man spirit, and unknown helps the child walk away from man and into truth. Let it go, let what is being held inside and that which was given to you with love from God go. Feel the cry inside and live, love, and give. Walk away free without being seen.

Seen and Unseen Change

When man can't be man in the flesh a search for love occurs. The world molds man into what is necessary for society. When man seeks the unknown, he becomes one and creates society.

To uncover truth, discipline rescues man and carries man to salvation. The just man pours out what's inside of man to the world. The just man changes for all that is good. The just man and his actions are the sweet sent that pleases God.

A New Challenge

The original man creates from within. Free to explore the world and give love, man unknown to his gift cries to be released. The reflection of what was given is seen and received. The soul prepares man to walk in full sight. To touch the heart of a neighbor, the reflection of man must be in truth. Physical, mental, and spiritual pain is blinded by the world and the unjust. The challenge is to walk away from temptations and begin to rebuild the soul of man. Failure occurs along the journey to all that is true.

Failure helps to rebuild the foundation of man that opens the door to reach God's will.

<u>Defiance</u>

A person must let go of the past to begin to find the inner self. Over and over again a close friend reminds man of what used to be. Man must discover that which exists beyond death in order to gain eternal sight.

When man walks away from God because of what's seen by the naked eye, defiance of all that is true occurs. Defiance is sometimes needed for man to find man which ultimately seeks and find all that is true.

Eternity: Built from within love loves.

Passion withstands truth and delivers peace.

Thoughts, actions, and beliefs build a perfect storm.

A walk and vision nurtures love and the human experiences instant joy.

The universe and all that's created positions a revocable toy.

The spirit opens the door to create as created and life is discovered.

Eternity meets truth and truth needs no more.

The air is God's breath of love to the human.

When its Finished

Love exists and is given wholeheartedly from stranger to stranger. The closest friend is found from deep within. Truth carries life to all that was created. No hunger, no thirst, no pain, and no sorrow is seen. The being sends the scent of love from the heart that pleases God and transcends the seeking beings.

The end believes in the beginning. The beginning believes in the end. The everlasting seeks the God of gods- The God of Abraham, Isaac, and Jacob; and lives when it's finished.

Relationships

Love

      A slow dance that never ends is the thought that occurs when man gives true love and receives it in return. The emotions, feelings, and desires of the flesh are in the hands of the one that's loved. The excitement and pain that's felt by man prepares man to take the hand of God unconditionally. It is needed for man to seek the seen and unseen. The spirit builds strength to become one. The strong feelings that's experienced by man opens the heart and temporarily gives man the power of love as God. The person that receives the love chooses to accept or reject the love that's given. This in turn has man experience the acceptance or rejection of love that God feels.

      In order to love, the nature of the love that's given must be unconditional. Learning how to love unconditionally is the ultimate challenge of mankind. The love from man delivers the world to the universe and the unseen.

Indulgence

      Too much of anything causes the extreme individual to give

a caressing pain to man. It feels good but it hurts the being. As man ignores the signs that are loud and clear, The inner passion for salvation keeps the gift from the lord near. To believe the unbelievable puts man in the arms of the seen as its witnessed in the flesh. Messages, hints, and signs put all beliefs to the ultimate test.

Indulgence of what's seen in the world is needed because it develops the faith of man. Faith prepares man to take the hand of God without doubt. To defeat indulgence of any kind, man must give his will as its witnessed in the world to God. Listen and watch for the sign that provides true love and faith when the flesh of man is down and out.

Too Soon

Committing to something that a person is not prepared for is what causes pain. To make the journey unforgettable, man must believe in what is given from the heart by other to man.

Step by step God builds man. Step by step man builds himself with what is given. The journey of man begins and ends with belief. The feet that walk with man must be just and pleasing to the lord.

When the spirit cries the word of God is there to heal the

pain. Whether walking in or walking out, God gives love, guidance, and comfort to mankind for actions that are done too soon.

Being Ready

The energy of love enters man and takes full control of the desires within. Put your arms around God and hold on tight to what's created together. Being ready to give and receive true love helps man to discover God and God's will.

Willing and able the spirit within man blindly seeks truth within man. The challenge to connect two loves for eternity takes love from both. In order to touch the hand of God, man must give all his love to his neighbor and to himself. Loving unconditionally challenges man throughout every step of the journey. God gives the spirit. Spirit prepares man and what's given as true love to all.

The First Look

What is normally seen by man is not seen as true to the seeker. The illusion and rapture of false love traps the soul and limits what is given. Selfishly man wanders the world following what's been created by the naked eye.

Wherever man falsely goes, the spirit cries to be released to the world. The spirit yearns to deliver truth. The first look to a stranger becomes filled with love upon release of all that is true. The bottom becomes the top and man walks as living proof.

The everlasting cry is heard from the source to make what's happening right. Walk after walk prepares the vision of man to gain ultimate sight. Pillar after pillar is developed in the world only to miss the heart of man. The living being must learn to truly look at man's neighbor with love to experience the God created man.

Judging the Past

Looking to the past brings man closer to yesterday. Tomorrow exists because of the plans and actions of both the just and unjust. The past builds strength but also builds weakness.

Love explains the past. Happenings, hurt, and passions developed in the unseen ultimately to be delivered to all that is seen.

Man becomes weak when what's given from the past is not enough. While judging the past, the pain of sorrow after sorrow makes man sulk and wish for the end. Only to discover that the ones that is hurt is the closest friend within. Detaching from and understanding the past makes man able to grow. A just vision that's brought into being builds inner peace and gives true love to tomorrow.

Closest Friend

Never before seen is the power of love that's felt between man and his neighbor. Every thought, action, or happening is blessed with the whole heart. Half of a half, true friends walk to God in truth. Forgiveness of all sins is granted. The lord dwells within man and opens the door to what's breathing and deeply planted.

A stranger asks for love when it is absent. A Just man sees joy in hurt and pain while making a stranger love again. A closest friend makes man understand the power of love. As man sees the vision, man learns to love again and again.

Open Arms

Forgive with all heart and soul. Understand that love grows. To rescue love and forgive with a poured-out heart, deliver all that is true.

Test after test man passes to advance. What's missing is the why and everlasting mission to make man love.

Every gift that's given to man must be received with open

arms.   The spirit develops the being for all that is good in the universe. Life becomes because man puts his neighbor first.

The hidden power within man delivers the gift to man and to all that thirst.

A Message

<u>Learn, Grow, and Give Pure Love in All that You Do</u>

Imagination makes everything possible. The pain, hurt, and abandonment that's experienced makes man cry. Death after death, humiliation after humiliation has prepared man to experience what an ancestor had experienced and strived to give. Without looking back or forward, love lives and gives forever.

The man that learns to give all spirit, soul, and of man unconditionally as well as seeks truth, delivers the gift to the cry that's heard.

Deceit, hate, and all that is wrong that can be done to overpower another human being is never the choice. The being that chooses to hurt their neighbor mourns forever.

Love was born within man. It exists when man can't or doesn't want to be spirit, soul, or man.

As growth, occurs, man cries because of the journey. Seeking within propels the being and offers forgiveness to thee. Emotions create the soul. The soul uses the mind and the will to take action. Man controls the soul, emotions, mind, and the will.

The father is the water that nurtures all that is planted.

The air is God's breath of love to the human.

Foundations

Age Five- Lifelong Education Course

How to Complete the Module

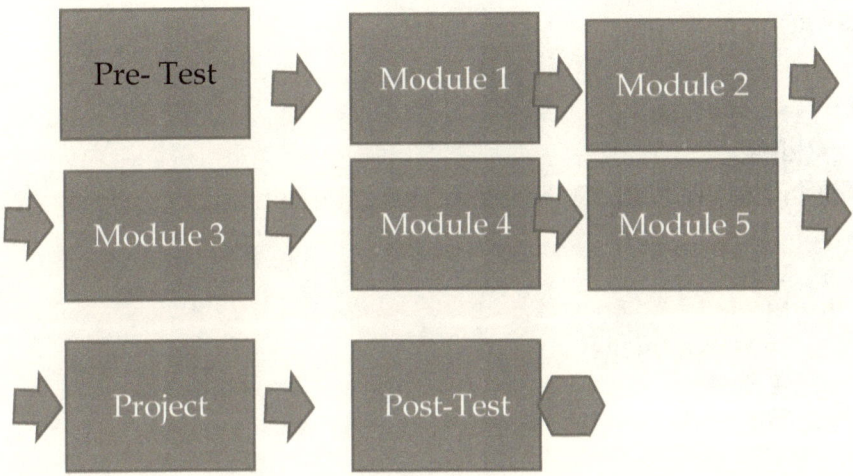

To complete the course and module, complete them in chronological order.

Pre-Test

Directions: Answer the twenty- five multiple choice questions. Use the answer key located at the end of the book to check your answers.

Question 1
What image did God of Abraham create the human?

    a. Water
    b. Moon
    c. His Own Image
    d. A Bird
    e. The Soil

Question 2
How many great lights did God create for the earth?

    a. 1
    b. 4
    c. 8
    d. 2
    e. 12

Question 3

How did the virgin Mary conceive Jesus ?

    a. Of the Holy Ghost
    b. Her Husband Joseph
    c. King David
    d. John the Baptist
    e. None of the Above

Question 4

Who did God of Abraham say he was when he spoke to Moses?

    a. I Go There
    b. I Am
    c. I See As Him
    d. I Do This Thing
    e. I Will Be Who I Will Be

Question 5

Who did Jesus say would rebuke the world of sin when he leaves?

    a. That Comforter
    b. John the Baptist
    c. The Pharisee
    d. Cesar
    e. None of the above

Question 6
What did God make the Human from?

    a. The Soil
    b. Different Animal Parts
    c. A Bird
    d. An Ape
    e. None of the above

Question 7
What thing beguiled the man and woman to eat from the tree they were commanded not to eat from?

    a. Dog
    b. Serpent
    c. Bird
    d. Cat
    e. Soil

Question 8
What is the sign of the covenant that God made with Noah that God will not create a flood to destroy the earth again?

    a. A Vinyard
    b. A Boat
    c. A Dove
    d. A Bow Set In The Clouds
    e. None of the Above

Question 9

What is the name of Abraham's son that Sarah gave birth to?

a. Jacob
b. Abraham
c. John
d. Joseph
e. Isaac

Question 10

What type of treasures did Jesus say to gather?

a. Diamonds
b. Treasures on earth
c. Treasurers to gather in heaven
d. Gold
e. Animals

Question 11

How old was Abram when he left the land of his birthplace?

a. 18
b. 30
c. 50
d. 99
e. 75

Question 12

Jesus explains that being and believing like what is the greatest in Heaven?

    a. King
    b. Pharise
    c. Spirit
    d. Child
    e. Disciple

Question 13

What did Jesus do for his disciples that he said they should do to others?

    a. Caught Fish
    b. Washed Their Feet
    c. Took Them To Get Baptized
    d. Gave Them Gold
    e. Gave Them Land

Question 14

What day is a Sabbath day for the Lord God?

    a. First
    b. Third
    c. Second
    d. Seventh
    e. Sixth

Question 15

What did Jesus say to his eleven disciples when he saw them after rising from death?

    a. Hello
    b. Goodbye
    c. All power is given unto me in heaven and earth
    d. I have no power
    e. None of the above

Question 16

Who did Joseph forgive when he was in Egypt?

    a. The people of the town
    b. The King
    c. His Father
    d. His Wife
    e. His Brothers

Question 17

Who knows all of the humans' thoughts?

    a. An Animal
    b. God
    c. The Disciples
    d. A Fortune Teller
    e. None of the Above

Question 18

Who does Jesus Christ Honor?

    a. Gold
    b. Silver
    c. Cesar
    d. The Father
    e. Animals

Question 19

When saying "The Lord's Prayer", what should be fulfilled on earth as it is in Heaven?

    a. Greed
    b. Happiness
    c. Hate
    d. Wealth and Power
    e. God's Will

Question 20

What advice did King Solomon give to his son?

    a. Gain all power in the land
    b. Gather gold, silver, and oil
    c. Trust in the Lord with all your heart
    d. Own as many animals as you can
    e. None of the above

Question 21
What does God tell Moses about any human that sees his face?

a. They will be happy
b. They will fly like a bird
c. They will swim like a fish
d. They will not see his face and live
e. They will become wealthy

Question 22
What foundation did Paul speak about adding to?

a. A house
b. Cesar
c. John the Baptists
d. Peter
e. Jesus Christ

Question 23
Why did God free the Israelites from Egypt?

a. Because of the covenant he made with Abraham, Isaac, and Jacob
b. Because of the King of Egypt
c. Because there was no one to work the land
d. Because of Moses
e. Because of the covenant he made with the King of Egypt.

Question 24

What does Jesus say he is as long as he is in the world?

    a. The star of the world
    b. The wealthiest of the world
    c. The dark of the world
    d. The light of the world
    e. The poorest of the world

Question 25

What does Jesus say that every man should do that goes before God?

    a. Sing
    b. Cry
    c. Give him gold, land, and oil
    d. Humble themselves and give praise
    e. Run and hide

Chapter 1

Module 1

Module 1

Identify three ways to answer the question " Who Am I As A Person Living On Earth?"

Overview of Module 1

In this module individuals will explore the foundations of spirituality and the human living in the world. Individuals will gain knowledge of the God of Abraham, Jesus Christ, and the Holy Spirit.

Strength Within Man

The Lord's love conquers all.

Man was built with loves image despite the fall.

Life overcomes and wrongs become right.

To see God in man illuminates truth.

Man must seek truth to plant the seeds and flowers of youth.

By Dawei

The following outcomes will be the focus of this module:

Module 1: Learning Outcome 1- Demonstrate knowledge of spirituality.

Module 1: Learning Outcome 2-Demonstrate knowledge of what is known that makes up the planet earth.

Module 1: Learning Outcome 3-Demonstrate knowledge of God.

Module 1: Learning Outcome 4- Demonstrate knowledge of Jesus Christ.

Module 1: Learning Outcome 5- Demonstrate knowledge of the Holy Spirit.

Module 1: Learning Outcome 1

Demonstrate knowledge of spirituality.

Overview of Module 1: Learning Outcome 1

The human lives on earth. The spirit lives in the human. The earth is made up of many different humans. All humans share the same source of love. God of Abraham is the creator of all. Jesus Christ is the son of the God of Abraham. The Holy Ghost is the power and living source of the God of Abraham.

Module 1 Learning Outcome 1 Reading #1

Title: Bible- Genesis Chapter 1 Verses 26-31

Introduction:

God of Abraham created the human in his image.

Written Verses:

Verse 26-

Good. And God said, "Let us make a human in our image, by our likeness, to hold sway over the fish of the sea and the fowl of the heavens and the cattle and the wild beast and all the crawling things that crawl upon the earth.

Verse 27-

And God created the human in his image, in the image of God He created him, male and female he created them.

Verse 28-

And God blessed them, and God said to them, "Be fruitful and multiply and fill the earth and conquer it, and hold sway over the fish of the sea and

Verse 29-

the fowl of the heavens and every beast that crawls upon the earth." And God said, "Look, I have given you every seed-bearing plant on the face of all the earth and every tree that has fruit

bearing seed, yours they will be

Verse 30-

for food. And to all the beasts of the earth and to all the fowl of

the heavens and to all that crawls on the earth, which has the

breath of life within

Verse 31-

it, the green plants for food." And so it was. And God saw that he

had done, and, look, it was very good. And it was evening and its

was morning, the sixth day.

Module 1 Learning Outcome 1 Reading #2

Title: Bible- Genesis Chapter 1 Verses 1-6

Introduction:

God of Abraham created heaven and earth.

Written Verses:

Verse 1-

When God began to create heaven and earth,

Verse 2-

And the earth then was welter and waste and darkness over the

deep and

Verse 3-

God's breath hovering over the waters, God said, "Let there be

light." And

Verse 4-

There was light. And God saw the light, that it was good, and God

divided

Verse 5-

the light from the darkness. And God called the light day, and the

darkness

Verse 6-

He called night. And it was evening and it was morning, first day.

And God said, "Let there be a vault in the midst of the waters, and

let it divide water.

Written Thought Response Assignment for Module 1 Learning Outcome 1

Directions:

Read both module learning outcome readings. Then provide your own original thoughts based on what you read. Use the suggested guide below to help you gather your thoughts.

- Think about what you liked about both readings.
- Think about what you didn't like about both readings.
- Think about what was interesting to you about both readings.

After thinking about the above suggested guides, write and summarize your final thoughts about both readings in six (6) sentences or less.

Write Your Final Thoughts for Module 1 Learning Outcome 1 In the Space Below:

Sentence 1-

Sentence 2-

Sentence 3-

Sentence 4-

Sentence 5-

Sentence- 6-

Module 1: Learning Outcome 2

Demonstrate knowledge of what is known that makes up the planet earth.

Overview of Module 1: Learning Outcome 2

In this learning outcome individuals will examine how the earth was created. Individuals will gain knowledge of what makes up earth.

Module 1 Learning Outcome 2 Reading #1

Title: Bible- Genesis Chapter 1 Verses 7-12

Introduction:

God of Abraham created the earth, seas, plants, and trees.

Written Verses:

Verse 7-

From water". And God made the vault and it divided the water beneath the

Verse 8-

vault from the water above the vault, and so it was. And God called the vault

Verse 9-

Heavens, and it was evening and it was morning, second day. And God said, "Let the waters under the heavens be gathered in one place so that the dry

Verse 10-

land will appear," and so it was. And God called the dry land Earth and the

Verse 11-

Gathering of waters He called Seas, and God saw that it was good.

And God said, "Let the earth grow grass, plants yielding seed of each kind and trees bearing fruit of each kind, that has its seed within it upon the earth." And so

Verse 12-

it was. And the earth put forth grass, plants yielding seed, and trees bearing

Module 1 Learning Outcome 2 Reading #2

Title: Bible- Genesis Chapter 1 Verses 13-18

Introduction:

God of Abraham created light for the day and light for the night.

Written Verses:

Verse 13-

fruit of each kind, and God saw that it was good. And it was evening and

Verse 14-

it was morning, third day. And God said, "Let there be lights in the vault of the heavens to divide the day from the night, and they shall be signs for

Verse 15-

the fixed times and for days and years, and they shall be lights in the vault

Verse 16-

of the heavens to light up the earth." And so it was. And God made the two great lights, the great light for dominion of the day and the small light for

Verse 17-

dominion of night, and the stars. And God placed them in the vault

of the

Verse 18-

heavens to light up the earth and to have dominion over day and

night and

Written Thought Response Assignment for Module 1 Learning Outcome 2

Directions:

Read both module learning outcome readings. Then provide your own original thoughts based on what you read. Use the suggested guide below to help you gather your thoughts.

- Think about what you liked about both readings.
- Think about what you didn't like about both readings.
- Think about what was interesting to you about both readings.

After thinking about the above suggested guides, write and summarize your final thoughts about both readings in six (6) sentences or less.

Write Your Final Thoughts for Module 1 Learning Outcome 2 In The Space Below:

Sentence 1-

Sentence 2-

Sentence 3-

Sentence 4-

Sentence 5-

Sentence- 6-

Module 1: Learning Outcome 3

Demonstrate knowledge of God.

Overview of Module 1: Learning Outcome 3

In this learning outcome individuals will examine our creator God. Individuals will examine Gods words that are spoken to individuals living on earth. Individuals will gain knowledge of the God of Abraham.

Module 1 Learning Outcome 3 Reading #1

Title: Bible- Genesis Chapter 17 Verses 1-6

Introduction:

God of Abraham speaks to Abraham.

Written Verses:

Verse 1-

And Abram was ninety-nine years old, and the Lord appeared to

Abram and said to him, "I am El Shaddai. Walk in My

Verse 2-

Presence and be blameless, and I will grant my covenant between

Me and

Verse 3-

You and I will multiply you very greatly." And Abram flung himself

on his

Verse 4-

Face, and God spoke to him, saying, "As for Me, this is My

covenant with

Verse 5-

You: you shall be father to a multitude of nations. And no longer

shall your name be called Abram but your name shall be Abraham, for l have made

Verse 6-

you father to a multitude of nations. And l will make you most abundantly fruitful and turn you into nations, and kings shall come forth from you.

Module 1 Learning Outcome 3 Reading #2

Title: Bible- Exodus Chapter 3 Verses 10-15

Introduction:

God of Abraham speaks to Moses

Written Verses:

Verse 10-

Which the Egyptians oppress them. And now, go that I may send you to

Verse 11-

Pharaoh, and bring My people the Israelites out of Egypt." And Moses said to God, "Who am I that I should go to Pharaoh and that I should bring out

Verse 12-

The Israelites from Egypt?" And He said, "For I will be with you. And this is the sign for you that I Myself have sent you. When you bring the people out from Egypt, you shall worship God on this mountain." And Moses said

Verse 13-

To God, "Look, when I come to the Israelites and say to them, "The God of your fathers has sent me to you," and they say to me,

"What is His name?,"

Verse 14-

what shall I say to them?" And God said to Moses, "Ehyeh-'Asher-'Ehyeh, I-Will-Be-Who-I-Will-Be." And He said, "Thus shall you say to the Israel-

Verse 15-

ites, ' 'Ehyeh has sent me to you.'" The Lord God of your fathers, the God of Abraham, the God of Isaac, and the God of Jacob, sent me to you.

That is My name forever

and thus am I invoked in all ages.'

Written Thought Response Assignment for Module 1 Learning Outcome 3

Directions:

Read both module learning outcome readings. Then provide your own original thoughts based on what you read. Use the suggested guide below to help you gather your thoughts.

- Think about what you liked about both readings.
- Think about what you didn't like about both readings.
- Think about what was interesting to you about both readings.

After thinking about the above suggested guides, write and summarize your final thoughts about both readings in six (6) sentences or less.

Write Your Final Thoughts for Module 1 Learning Outcome 3 In the Space Below:

Sentence 1-

Sentence 2-

Sentence 3-

Sentence 4-

Sentence 5-

Sentence- 6-

Module 1: Learning Outcome 4

Demonstrate knowledge of Jesus Christ.

Overview of Module 1: Learning Outcome 4

In this learning outcome individuals will examine the son of God, Jesus Christ. Individuals will examine Jesus's birth and baptism.

Module 1 Learning Outcome 4 Reading #1

Title: The New Testament Bible- The Gospel of Mathew Chapter 1

Introduction:

The Conceiving of Jesus.

Written Gospel:

Writing 1-

Then her husband Joseph being a perfect man/ and loth to defame her/ was mined to put her away secretly.

Writing 2-

While he thus thought/

Writing 3-

Behold the Angel of the lord appeared onto him in sleep saying: Joseph the son of David/ fear not to take onto the/ Mary thy wife.

Writing 4-

For that which is conceived in her is of the holy ghost.

Writing 5-

She shall bring forth a son/ and thou shalt call his name Jesus.

Writing 6-

For he shall save his people from their sins.

Module 1 Learning Outcome 4 Reading #2

Title: The New Testament Bible- The Gospel of Mathew Chapter 3

Introduction:

The Baptism of Jesus.

Written Gospel:

Writing 1-

But John forbade him/ saying: I ought to be baptized of the: and comest you to me:

Writing 2-

Jesus answered and said to him: Let it be so now. For thus it becometh as to fulfill all righteousness.

Writing 3-

Then he suffered him.

Writing 4-

And Jesus as soon as he was baptized/came straight out of the water:

Writing 5-

And lo heaven was open onto him: and he saw the spirit of God descend like a dove/ and light upon him.

Writing 6-

And lo there came a voice from heaven saying: This is my dear son whom is my delight.

Written Thought Response Assignment for Module 1 Learning Outcome 4

Directions:

Read both module learning outcome readings. Then provide your own original thoughts based on what you read. Use the suggested guide below to help you gather your thoughts.

- Think about what you liked about both readings.
- Think about what you didn't like about both readings.
- Think about what was interesting to you about both readings.

After thinking about the above suggested guides, write and summarize your final thoughts about both readings in six (6) sentences or less.

Write Your Final Thoughts for Module 1 Learning Outcome 4 In The Space Below:

Sentence 1-

Sentence 2-

Sentence 3-

Sentence 4-

Sentence 5-

Sentence- 6-

Module 1: Learning Outcome 5

Demonstrate knowledge of the Holy Spirit.

Overview of Module 1: Learning Outcome 5

In this learning outcome individuals will examine the Holy Spirit.

Module 1 Learning Outcome 5 Reading #1

Title:

Bible- Exodus Chapter 32 Verses 32-35

Bible- Exodus Chapter 33 Verses 1-2

Introduction:

God of Abraham speaks to Moses.

Written Gospel:

Verse 32-

selves gods of gold. And now, if You would bear their offense...,
and if not,

Verse 33-

Wipe me out, pray, from your book which You have written." And
the Lord said to Moses, "He who has offended against Me, I shall
wipe him out from

Verse 34-

My book. And now, lead this people to where I have spoken to you.
Look, My messenger shall go before you. And on the day I make
reckoning, I will

Verse 35-

Make a reckoning with them for their offense." And the Lord

scourged the people for having made the calf that Aaron made.

Verse 1-

And the Lord said to Moses, "Go, head up from here, you and the

people that you brought up from the land of Egypt, to the land that

I swore to Abraham, to Isaac, and to Jacob, saying, "To

Verse 2-

your seed I will give it." And I shall send a messenger before you

and I shall drive out the Canaanite, the Amorite, and the Hittite and

the Perizzite,

Module 1 Learning Outcome 5 Reading #2

Title: The New Testament Bible- The Gospel of John Chapter 16

Introduction:

Jesus speaking and explaining why he must go away.

Written Gospel:

Writing 1-

But, now go l my way to him that sent me/ and none of you asketh me; whither goest thou:

Writing 2-

but because l have said such things unto you/ your hearts are full of sorrow.

Writing 3-

Nevertheless l tell you the truth it is expedient for you that l go away.

Writing 4-

For if l go not away/ that comforter will not come unto you.

Writing 5-

If l depart l will send him unto you. And when he is come/ he will rebuke the world of sin/ and of righteousness, and of judgement.

Writing 6-

Of sin/because they believe not on me: of righteousness/ because

I go to my father/ and ye shall see me no more: And of

judgement/because the chief ruler of this world/is judged already.

Written Thought Response Assignment for Module 1 Learning Outcome 5

Directions:

Read both module learning outcome readings. Then provide your own original thoughts based on what you read. Use the suggested guide below to help you gather your thoughts.

- Think about what you liked about both readings.
- Think about what you didn't like about both readings.
- Think about what was interesting to you about both readings.

After thinking about the above suggested guides, write and summarize your final thoughts about both readings in six (6) sentences or less.

Write Your Final Thoughts for Module 1 Learning Outcome 5 In the Space Below:

Sentence 1-

Sentence 2-

Sentence 3-

Sentence 4-

Sentence 5-

Sentence- 6-

Module 1 Vocabulary Assignment

Directions:

Each module you will define three (3) words that are mentioned or relevant to the topics discussed within the module. Use the end of the book to read the author's definition of word that's listed, then search, find, and read the word using a different source such as (book, individual, computer), and then finally write the definition in your own words.

Choose from the following list of words for Module 1:

God of Abraham
Jesus Christ
Holy Ghost
Holy Spirit
Planet
Earth
Day
Night
Spirituality

<u>Word #1:</u>

Author's Definition:

Source Definition:

Your Definition:

<u>Word #2:</u>

Author's Definition:

Source Definition:

Your Definition:

Word #3:

Author's Definition:

Source Definition:

Your Definition:

Chapter 2

Module 2

Module 2

Apply critical thinking skills to answer the question "Why Am I Here On Earth?"

Overview of Module 2

In this module individuals will explore the human living on earth.

Belief in all that is true brings the being to ponder the question "why am I here on earth?". The earth was created by the God of Abraham for the God of Abraham. The kingdoms created by God extends love to the individual that wholeheartedly believe, seek, and give as God.

Father

Begin to feel the Father's every word.

It will take a while to understand life's wandering curve.

To give life to all living things requires nurturing.

To receive as well as give the father builds from the heart.

When in need the Son seeks the Father.

When lost the Son finds the Father.

Love unites the Father and the Son as the tide begins to rise.

The Gift to the world becomes the ultimate prize.

The Son was born with a given purpose.

Love from the Father gives the Son guidance and a pleasing sent.

A Father believes, leads, gives, nurtures, and serves.

A Son receives, grows, understands, unites, and begins to deserve.

By Dawei

The following outcomes will be the focus of this module:

Module 2: Learning Outcome 6- Demonstrate an understanding of the basic attributes required to be a living human being on earth.

Module 2: Learning Outcome 7-Demonstrate an understanding of how a living human being is born.

Module 2: Learning Outcome 8-Demonstrate an understanding of the emotions of love and hate.

Module 2: Learning Outcome 9- Demonstrate knowledge of an individual innate special talent or gift.

Module 2: Learning Outcome 10- Demonstrate knowledge of an individual purpose.

Module 2: Learning Outcome 6

Demonstrate an understanding of the basic attributes required to be a living human being on earth.

Overview of Module 2: Learning Outcome 6

In this learning outcome individuals will examine how the human was created by God of Abraham. Individuals will gain knowledge of what makes each human blessed, gifted, special, and unique.

Module 2 Learning Outcome 6 Reading #1

Title: Bible- Genesis Chapter 2 Verses 4-9

Introduction:

God of Abraham creates the human man.

Written Verses:

Verse 4-

all His task that He had created to do. This is the tale of the heavens and earth when they were created.

Verse 5-

On the day the Lord God made earth and heavens, no shrub of the field being yet on the earth and no plant of the field yet sprouted, for the Lord God had not caused rain to fall on earth and there was no human to

Verse 6-

till the soil, and wetness would well from the earth to water all the surface

Verse 7-

of the soil, then the Lord God fashioned the human, humus from the soil, and blew into his nostrils the breath of life, and the human became a living

Verse 8-

creature. And the Lord God planted a garden in Eden, to the east, and

Verse 9-

He placed there the human He had fashioned. And the Lord God caused to sprout from the soil every tree lovely to look at and good for food, and the tree of life was in the midst of the garden, and the tree of knowledge,

Module 2 Learning Outcome 6 Reading #2

Title: Bible- Genesis Chapter 2 Verses 18-23

Introduction:

God of Abraham creates the human woman.

Written Verses:

Verse 18-

And the Lord God said, "It is not good for the human to be alone,

I shall

Verse 19-

make him a sustainer beside him." And the Lord God fashioned

from the soil each beast of the field and each fowl of the heavens

and brought each to the human to see what he would call it, and

whatever the human called

Verse 20-

a living creature, that was its name. And the human called names

to all the cattle and to the fowl of the heavens and to all the beasts

of the field, but for

Verse 21-

the human no sustainer beside him was found. And the Lord God

cast a deep slumber on the human, and he slept, and He took one

of his ribs and

Verse 22-

closed over the flesh where it had been, and the Lord God build

the rib He had taken from the human into a woman and he brought

her to the human.

Verse 23-

And the human said:

"This one at last, bone of my bones and flesh of my flesh, "This

one shall be called Woman, for from man was this one taken."

Written Thought Response Assignment for Module 2 Learning Outcome 6

Directions:

Read both module learning outcome readings. Then provide your own original thoughts based on what you read. Use the suggested guide below to help you gather your thoughts.

- Think about what you liked about both readings.
- Think about what you didn't like about both readings.
- Think about what was interesting to you about both readings.

After thinking about the above suggested guides, write and summarize your final thoughts about both readings in six (6) sentences or less.

Write Your Final Thoughts for Module 2 Learning Outcome 6 In the Space Below:

Sentence 1-

Sentence 2-

Sentence 3-

Sentence 4-

Sentence 5-

Sentence- 6-

Module 2: Learning Outcome 7

Demonstrate an understanding of how a living human being is born.

Overview of Module 2: Learning Outcome 7

In this learning outcome individuals will examine how the human is born through a woman. Individuals will gain knowledge of man and woman.

Module 2 Learning Outcome 7 Reading #1

Title: Bible- Genesis Chapter 3 Verses 8-13

Introduction:

The human man and the human woman hide from God of Abraham.

Written Verses:

Verse 8-

And they heard the sound of the Lord God walking about in the garden in the evening breeze, and the human and his woman hid from the Lord

Verse 9-

God in the midst of the trees of the garden. And the Lord God called to

Verse 10-

the human and said to him, "Where are you?" And he said, "I heard Your

Verse 11-

sound in the garden and I was afraid, for I was naked, and I hid." And He said, "Who told you that you were naked? From the tree I commanded you

---

Verse 12-

not to eat have you eaten? And the human said, "The woman whom you

Verse 13-

gave by me, she gave me from the tree, and I ate." And the Lord God said to the woman, "What is this you have done?" And the woman said, "The

Module 2 Learning Outcome 7 Reading #2

Title: Bible- Genesis Chapter 3 Verses 14-19

Introduction:

God of Abraham speaks to the serpent, the woman, and the human man.

Written Verses:

Verse 14-

serpent beguiled me and I ate." And the Lord God said to the serpent, Because you have done this,

Cursed be you of all cattle and all beasts of the field. On your belly shall you go and dust shall you eat all the days of your life.

Verse 15-

Enmity will I set between you and the woman, between your seed and hers. He will bite your head and you will boot him with the heel."

Verse 16-

To the woman he said,

"I will terribly sharpen your birth pangs, in pain shall you bear children. And for your man shall be your longing, and he shall rule over you."

Verse 17-

And to the human he said, "Because you listened to the voice of your wife and ate from the tree that I commanded you, "You shall not eat from it,'

Cursed be the soil for your sake, with pangs shall you eat from it all the days of your life.

Verse 18-

Thorn and thistle shall it sprout for you and you shall eat the plants of the field.

Verse 19-

By the sweat of your brow shall you eat bread till you return to the soil, for from there you were taken, for dust you are and to dust shall you return."

Written Thought Response Assignment for Module 2 Learning Outcome 7

Directions:

Read both module learning outcome readings. Then provide your own original thoughts based on what you read. Use the suggested guide below to help you gather your thoughts.

- Think about what you liked about both readings.
- Think about what you didn't like about both readings.
- Think about what was interesting to you about both readings.

After thinking about the above suggested guides, write and summarize your final thoughts about both readings in six (6) sentences or less.

Write Your Final Thoughts for Module 2 Learning Outcome 7 In The Space Below:

Sentence 1-

Sentence 2-

Sentence 3-

Sentence 4-

Sentence 5-

Sentence- 6-

Module 2: Learning Outcome 8

Demonstrate an understanding of the emotions of love and hate.

Overview of Module 2: Learning Outcome 8

In this learning outcome individuals will examine how the emotions of love and hate both builds and ends life. Individuals will gain knowledge of prayer, forgiveness, and making a promise when feeling the emotions of love or hate.

Module 2 Learning Outcome 8 Reading #1

Title: Bible- Genesis Chapter 9 Verses 9-14

Introduction:

God promises not to over flood the earth again because of the human.

Written Verses:

Verse 9-

And God said to Noah and to his sons with him, "And l, l am about to

Verse 10-

establish My covenant with you and with your seed after you, and with every living creature that is with you, the fowl and the cattle and every beast of the

Verse 11-

earth. "And l will establish My covenant with you, that never again shall all flesh be cut off by the waters of the Flood, and never again shall there be a

Verse 12-

Flood to destroy the earth." And God said, "This is the sign of the

covenant that I set between Me and you and every living creatures

that is with you, for

Verse 13-

everlasting generations: My bow I have set in the clouds to be a

sign of the

Verse 14-

covenant between Me and the earth, and so, when I send clouds

over the

Module 2 Learning Outcome 8 Reading #2

Title: The New Testament Bible- The Gospel of Mathew Chapter 6

Introduction:

How to Pray: Prayer from Jesus Christ

Written Verses:

Writing 1-

Verily I say unto you/ they have their reward.

Writing 2-

But when thou prayest/ enter into thy chamber/ and shut the door to thee/ and pray to thy father which is in secret: and thy father which seeith in secret/ shall reward thee openly.

Writing 3-

But when ye pray/ babble not much/ as the gentils do: for they think that they shall be heard/ for their much babblings sake.

Writing 4-

Be ye not like them therefore.

Writing 5-

For your father knoweth where of ye have need/ before ye ask of him.

Writing 6-

After this manner therefore pray ye

Written Thought Response Assignment for Module 2 Learning Outcome 8

Directions:

Read both module learning outcome readings. Then provide your own original thoughts based on what you read. Use the suggested guide below to help you gather your thoughts.

- Think about what you liked about both readings.
- Think about what you didn't like about both readings.
- Think about what was interesting to you about both readings.

After thinking about the above suggested guides, write and summarize your final thoughts about both readings in six (6) sentences or less.

Write Your Final Thoughts for Module 2 Learning Outcome 8 In The Space Below:

Sentence 1-

Sentence 2-

Sentence 3-

Sentence 4-

Sentence 5-

Sentence- 6-

Module 2: Learning Outcome 9

Demonstrate knowledge of an individual innate special talent or gift.

Overview of Module 2: Learning Outcome 9

In this learning outcome individuals will examine innate talents and gifts. Individuals will gain knowledge of what treasures to gather.

Module 2 Learning Outcome 9 Reading #1

Title: The New Testament Bible- The Gospel of Mathew Chapter

6

Introduction:

Jesus explains what treasures to gather.

Written Verses:

Writing 1-

Gather not treasure together on earth/ where rust and moths

corrupt/ and where thieves break through and steal.

Writing 2-

But gather ye treasure to gather in heaven/ where neither rust/

nor moths corrupt.

Writing 3-

And where thieves neither break up/ nor yet steal.

Writing 4-

For wheresoever your treasure is there are your heart also.

Writing 5-

The light of thy body is thine eye.

Writing 6-

Wherefore if thine eye be single/ all thy body is full of light but and
if thine eye be wicked/ then is all thy body full of darkness.

Module 2 Learning Outcome 9 Reading #2

Title: Bible- Genesis Chapter 17 Verses 16-21

Introduction:

God establishes a covenant with Isaac upon birth.

Written Verses:

Verse 16-

is her name. And I will bless her and I will also give you from her

a son and I will bless him, and she shall become nations, kings of

people shall

Verse 17-

Issue from her." And Abraham flung himself on his face and he

laughed, saying to himself,

To a hundred-year-old will a child be born, will ninety-year-old

Sarah give birth?"

Verse 18-

And Abraham said to God, "Would that Ishmael might live in Your

favor!"

Verse 19-

And God said, "Yet Sarah your wife is to bear you a son and you shall call his name Isaac and I will establish My covenant with him as an everlast-

Verse 20-

-ing covenant, for his seed after him. As for Ishmael, I have heard you. Look, I will bless him and make him fruitful and will multiply him most abundantly, twelve chieftains he shall beget, and I will make him a great

Verse 21-

Nation. But My covenant I will establish with Isaac whom Sarah will bear

Written Thought Response Assignment For Module 2 Learning Outcome 9

Directions:

Read both module learning outcome readings. Then provide your own original thoughts based on what you read. Use the suggested guide below to help you gather your thoughts.

- Think about what you liked about both readings.
- Think about what you didn't like about both readings.
- Think about what was interesting to you about both readings.

After thinking about the above suggested guides, write and summarize your final thoughts about both readings in six (6) sentences or less.

Write Your Final Thoughts for Module 2 Learning Outcome 9 In The Space Below:

Sentence 1-

Sentence 2-

Sentence 3-

Sentence 4-

Sentence 5-

Sentence- 6-

Module 2: Learning Outcome 10

Demonstrate knowledge of an individual purpose.

Overview of Module 2: Learning Outcome 10

In this learning outcome individuals will examine individual purposes. Individuals gain knowledge of inner voices and feelings.

Module 2 Learning Outcome 10 Reading #1

Title: The New Testament Bible- The Gospel of John Chapter 16

Introduction:

Jesus explains why he must go back to him that sent him

Written Verses:

Writing 1-

But, now go l my way to him that sent me/ and none of you asketh

me; whither goest thou;

Writing 2-

but because l have said such things unto you/ your hearts are full

of sorrow.

Writing 3-

Nevertheless l tell you the truth it is expedient for you that l go

away.

Writing 4-

For if l go not away/ that comforter will not come unto you.

Writing 5-

And when he is come/ he will rebuke the world of sin/ and of

righteousness, and of judgement.

Writing 6-

of sin/ because they believe not on me; Of righteousness/ because

I go to my father/ and ye shall see me no more: And of

judgement/ because the chief ruler of this world/ is judged

already.

Module 2 Learning Outcome 10 Reading #2

Title: Bible- Genesis Chapter 12 Verses 1-6

Introduction:

God tells Abram to leave the land of his birthplace.

Written Verses:

Verse 1-

And the Lord said to Abram, "Go forth from your land and your birthplace and your father's house to the land I will

Verse 2-

show you. And I will make you a great nation and I will bless you and make

Verse 3-

your name great, and you shall be a blessing. And I will bless those who bless you, and those who damn you I will curse, and all the clans of the

Verse 4-

Earth through you shall be blessed." And Abram went forth as the Lord had spoken to him and Lot went forth with him, Abram being seventy-five

Verse 5-

years old when he left Haran. And Abram took Sarai his wife and

Lot his nephew and all the goods they had gotten and the folk they

had bought in Haran, and they set out on the way to the land of

Canaan, and they came

Verse 6-

to the land of Canaan. And Abram crossed through the land to the

site of Shechem, to the Terebinth of Moreh. The Canaanite was

then in the land.

Written Thought Response Assignment for Module 2 Learning Outcome 10

Directions:

Read both module learning outcome readings. Then provide your own original thoughts based on what you read. Use the suggested guide below to help you gather your thoughts.

- Think about what you liked about both readings.
- Think about what you didn't like about both readings.
- Think about what was interesting to you about both readings.

After thinking about the above suggested guides, write and summarize your final thoughts about both readings in six (6) sentences or less.

Write Your Final Thoughts for Module 2 Learning Outcome 10 In The Space Below:

Sentence 1-

Sentence 2-

Sentence 3-

Sentence 4-

Sentence 5-

Sentence- 6-

Module 2 Vocabulary Assignment

Directions:

Each module you will define three (3) words that are mentioned or relevant to the topics discussed within the module. Use the end of the book to read the author's definition of word that's listed, then search, find, and read the word using a different source such as (book, individual, computer), and then finally write the definition in your own words.

Choose from the following list of words for Module 2:

Water
Air
Living
Human
Human Senses

Word #1:

Author's Definition:

Source Definition:

Your Definition:

Word #2:

Author's Definition:

Source Definition:

Your Definition:

<u>Word #3:</u>

Author's Definition:

Source Definition:

Your Definition:

Chapter 3

Module 3

Module 3

Describe three strategies to answer the question "What Can I do As a Person Living on Earth?"

Overview of Module 3

This module explores the human and the roles the human take on to sustain the earth.

Harness the gift that's planted inside of the human. The pain and joy to develop and deliver all that is true is up to you. Nurturing the self begins with seeking all that is true. Truth exposes the self. Upon discovery the being begins to create.

A Cry to the Lord

Walk with me forever.

The soul wanders without seeking cover.

Unaware and lonely the soul of man cries.

Day after day a subtle vision of the Kingdom of Heaven opens the eyes.

The promise granted by the commands sparks the fire.

To give to man when man doesn't know man shows your presence.

To build together opens life as man, spirit, and love creates a tomorrow that's heaven sent.

To fall, to rise, and to begin happens through truth.

Freely the spirit builds man as tears felt by the Lord is proof.

By Dawei

The following outcomes will be the focus of this module:

Module 3: Learning Outcome 11- Demonstrate knowledge of how an individual can help themselves.

Module 3: Learning Outcome 12-Demonstrate knowledge of how an individual can help their family.

Module 3: Learning Outcome 13-Demonstrate knowledge of how an individual can help their community.

Module 3: Learning Outcome 14- Demonstrate knowledge of how an individual can help their country.

Module 3: Learning Outcome 15- Demonstrate knowledge of how an individual can help the world.

Module 3: Learning Outcome 11

Demonstrate knowledge of how an individual can help themselves.

Overview of Module 3: Learning Outcome 11

In this learning outcome individuals will examine the sabbath day that the God of Abraham established. Individuals will gain knowledge of being and believing as a child.

Module 3 Learning Outcome 11 Reading #1

Title: Bible- Exodus Chapter 16 Verses 21-26

Introduction:

Moses explains the holy sabbath day of the lord.

Written Verses:

Verse 21-

And they gathered it morning after morning every man according

to what

Verse 22-

He must eat, and when the sun grew hot, it melted. And it

happened on the sixth day, that they gathered a double portion of

bread, two omers for each,

Verse 23-

and all the chiefs of the community came and told Moses. And he

said to them, "That is what the Lord has spoken. A day of rest, a

holy sabbath to the Lord is tomorrow. What you bake, bake, and

what you cook, cook, and whatever is left over leave for

yourselves to be kept until morning."

Verse 24-

And they left it until morning as Moses had charged, and it did not

stink,

Verse 25-

and there were no worms in it. And Moses said, "Eat it today, for

today is

Verse 26-

a sabbath to the Lord, today you will not find it in the field. Six

days you shall gather it, and on the seventh day, the sabbath, there

will be none then."

Module 3 Learning Outcome 11 Reading #2

Title: The New Testament Bible- The Gospel of Mathew Chapter 18

Introduction:

Jesus explains that being and believing like a child is the greatest in the Kingdom of Heaven.

Written Verses:

Writing 1-

The same time the disciples came onto Jesus saying: who is the greatest in the Kingdom of Heaven?

Writing 2-

Jesus called a child onto him/ and set him in the middle of them/ and said: verily I say onto you; except ye turn/ and become as children/ ye cannot enter the Kingdom of Heaven.

Writing 3-

Whosoever Therefore shall submit himself as this child/ he is the greatest in the Kingdom of Heaven.

Writing 4-

And whosoever receiveth such a child in my name/ receiveth me.

Writing 5-

But whosoever offend one of the little ones/ which believe in me:
it were better for him/ that a millstone were hanged about his
neck/ and that he were drowned in the depth of the see.

Writing 6-

Wo be onto the world because of evil occasions.

Written Thought Response Assignment for Module 3 Learning Outcome 11

Directions:

Read both module learning outcome readings. Then provide your own original thoughts based on what you read. Use the suggested guide below to help you gather your thoughts.

- Think about what you liked about both readings.
- Think about what you didn't like about both readings.
- Think about what was interesting to you about both readings.

After thinking about the above suggested guides, write and summarize your final thoughts about both readings in six (6) sentences or less.

Write Your Final Thoughts for Module 3 Learning Outcome 11 In The Space Below:

Sentence 1-

Sentence 2-

Sentence 3-

Sentence 4-

Sentence 5-

Sentence- 6-

Module 3: Learning Outcome 12

Demonstrate knowledge of how an individual can help their family.

Overview of Module 3: Learning Outcome 12

In this learning outcome individuals will examine forgiveness and love for family. Individuals will gain knowledge of how to serve all humans and give love.

Module 3 Learning Outcome 12 Reading #1

Title: Bible- Genesis Chapter 42 Verses 23-28

Introduction:

Joseph helps his brothers.

Written Verses:

Verse 23-

And they did not know that Joseph understood, for there was an interpreter

Verse 24-

Between them. And he turned away from them and wept and returned to them and spoke to them, and he took Simeon from them and placed him in fetters before their eyes.

Verse 25-

And Joseph gave orders to fill their baggage with grain and to put back their silver into each one's pack and to give them supplies for their way, and so he

Verse 26-

did for them. And they loaded their provisions on their donkeys and they

Verse 27-

set out from there. Then one of them opened his pack to give

provender to his donkey at the encampment, and he saw his silver

and, look, it was in

Verse 28-

the mouth of his bag. And he said to his brothers, "My silver has

been put back and, look, it's actually in my bag." And they were

dumbfounded and trembled each before his brother saying, "What

is this that God has done

Module 3 Learning Outcome 12 Reading #2

Title: The New Testament Bible- The Gospel of John Chapter 13

Introduction:

Jesus washes his disciples feet.

Written Verses:

Writing 1-

After had washed their feet/ and received his clothes/ and was set down again/ he said unto them: wot ye what I have done to you: ye call me master and lord/ and ye say well/ for so am I.

Writing 2-

If I then your lord and master have washed your feet/ ye also ought to wash one anothers feet.

Writing 3-

For I have given you an example/that ye should do as I have done to you.

Writing 4-

Verely verely I say unto you/ the servant is not greater then his master.

Writing 5-

Neither the messenger greater then he that sent him.

Writing 6-

If ye understand these things/ happy are ye if ye do them.

Written Thought Response Assignment for Module 3 Learning Outcome 12

Directions:

Read both module learning outcome readings. Then provide your own original thoughts based on what you read. Use the suggested guide below to help you gather your thoughts.

- Think about what you liked about both readings.
- Think about what you didn't like about both readings.
- Think about what was interesting to you about both readings.

After thinking about the above suggested guides, write and summarize your final thoughts about both readings in six (6) sentences or less.

Write Your Final Thoughts for Module 3 Learning Outcome 12 In The Space Below:

Sentence 1-

Sentence 2-

Sentence 3-

Sentence 4-

Sentence 5-

Sentence- 6-

Module 3: Learning Outcome 13

Demonstrate knowledge of how an individual can help their community.

Overview of Module 3: Learning Outcome 13

In this learning outcome individuals will examine God of Abrahams laws, festivals, and the sabbath day. Individuals will gain knowledge of how to keep the Sabbath day and God's laws that were given to Moses.

Module 3 Learning Outcome 13 Reading #1

Title: Bible- Leviticus Chapter 23 Verses 1-6

Introduction:

God speaks to Moses about the Sabbath Day and the Festival of Flatbread.

Written Verses:

Verse 1-

And the Lord spoke to Moses, saying, "Speak to the Israelites, and you shall say to them: "These are the fixed times of the Lord which you shall call sacred convocations.

Verse 2-

These are my fixed times.

Verse 3-

Six days shall tasks be done, and on the seventh day, an absolute sabbath, a sacred convocation. No task shall you do. It is a sabbath for the Lord

Verse 4-

in all your dwelling places. These are the fixed times of the Lord, sacred

Verse 5-

convocations which you shall call in their fixed time. In the first month on the fourteenth of the month at twilight a Passover offering to the Lord.

Verse 6-

And on the fifteenth day of this month, a Festival of Flatbread to the Lord.

Module 3 Learning Outcome 13 Reading #2

Title: The New Testament Bible- The Gospel of John Chapter 7

Introduction:

Jesus discusses the law that Moses received from God of Abraham about working on the Sabbath Day.

Written Verses:

Writing 1-

Did not Moses give you a law: And yet none of you keepeth the law: Why go ye about to kill me:

Writing 2-

The people answered and said: Thou hast the devil. Who goeth about to kill thee:

Writing 3-

Jesus answered/ and said unto them/ I have done one work/ and ye all marvel.

Writing 4-

Moses therefore gave unto you circumcision/ not because it is of Moses/ but of the fathers.

Writing 5-

And yet ye on the Sabbath Day circumcise a man.

Writing 6-

If a man on the Sabbath Day receive circumcision without breaking of the law of Moses: Disdain ye at me/ because I made a man every whit whole on the Sabbath Day: judge not after the utter appearance: but judge righteous judgement.

Written Thought Response Assignment for Module 3 Learning Outcome 13

Directions:

Read both module learning outcome readings. Then provide your own original thoughts based on what you read. Use the suggested guide below to help you gather your thoughts.

- Think about what you liked about both readings.
- Think about what you didn't like about both readings.
- Think about what was interesting to you about both readings.

After thinking about the above suggested guides, write and summarize your final thoughts about both readings in six (6) sentences or less.

Write Your Final Thoughts for Module 3 Learning Outcome 13 In The Space Below:

Sentence 1-

Sentence 2-

Sentence 3-

Sentence 4-

Sentence 5-

Sentence- 6-

Module 3: Learning Outcome 14

Demonstrate knowledge of how an individual can help their country.

Overview of Module 3: Learning Outcome 14

In this learning outcome individuals will examine how to plan, listen to God, and serve all humans. Individuals will gain knowledge of how humankind was saved.

Module 3 Learning Outcome 14 Reading #1

Title: Bible- Genesis Chapter 41 Verses 40-45

Introduction:

Pharaoh appoints Joseph as overseer over all the land of Egypt.

Written Verses:

Verse 40-

You shall be over my house, and by your lips all my folk shall be

guided. By

Verse 41-

the throne alone shall I be greater than you." And Pharaoh said to

Joseph,

Verse 42-

"See, I have set you over all the land of Egypt." And Pharaoh took

off his ring from his hand and put it on Joseph's hand and had him

clothed in fine

Verse 43-

linen clothes and placed the golden collar round his neck. And he

had him ride in the chariot of his viceroy, and they called out

before him Abrekh,

Verse 44-

Setting him over all the land of Egypt. And Pharaoh said to Joseph,

"I am Pharaoh! Without you no man shall raise hand or foot in all

the land of

Verse 45-

Egypt." And Pharaoh called Joseph's name Zaphenath-Paneah, and

he gave him Asenath daughter of Potiphera, priest of On, as wife,

and Joseph went out over the land of Egypt.

Module 3 Learning Outcome 14 Reading #2

Title: The New Testament Bible- The Gospel of Mathew Chapter 28

Introduction:

Jesus rises from the dead and speaks to his eleven disciples.

Written Verses:

Writing 1-

Then the eleven disciples went their way into galile/ into a mountain where Jesus had appointed them.

Writing 2-

And when they saw him/ they worshipped him.

Writing 3-

But some of them doubted.

Writing 4-

Jesus came and spoke unto them/ saying: All power is given unto me in heaven/ and earth.

Writing 5-

Go therefore and teach all nations/ baptizing them in the name of the father/ and the son/ and the Holy Ghost: teaching them to observe all things/ whatsoever I commanded you.

Writing 6-

And lo l am with you all way even until the end of the world.

Written Thought Response Assignment for Module 3 Learning Outcome 14

Directions:

Read both module learning outcome readings. Then provide your own original thoughts based on what you read. Use the suggested guide below to help you gather your thoughts.

- Think about what you liked about both readings.
- Think about what you didn't like about both readings.
- Think about what was interesting to you about both readings.

After thinking about the above suggested guides, write and summarize your final thoughts about both readings in six (6) sentences or less.

Write Your Final Thoughts for Module 3 Learning Outcome 14 In The Space Below:

Sentence 1-

Sentence 2-

Sentence 3-

Sentence 4-

Sentence 5-

Sentence- 6-

Module 3: Learning Outcome 15

Demonstrate knowledge of how an individual can help the world.

Overview of Module 3: Learning Outcome 15

In this learning outcome individuals will examine forgiveness of sin. Individuals will gain knowledge of how to give love to defeat sin.

Module 3 Learning Outcome 15 Reading #1

Title: Bible- Genesis Chapter 50 Verses 15-20

Introduction:

Joseph forgives his brothers.

Written Verses:

Verse 15-

And Joseph's brothers saw that their father was dead, and they said, "If

Verse 16-

Evil we caused him." And they charged Joseph, saying, "Your father left a

Verse 17-

charge his death, saying, 'Thus shall you say to Joseph, we beseech you, forgive, pray, the crime and the offense of your brothers, for evil they have caused you. And so now, forgive pray the crime of the servants of

Verse 18-

your father's God." And Joseph wept when they spoke to him. And

his brothers then came and flung themselves before him and said,

"Here we

Verse 19-

are, your slaves." And Joseph said, "Fear not, for am I instead of

God?

Verse 20-

While you meant evil toward me, God meant it for good, so as to

bring

Module 3 Learning Outcome 15 Reading #2

Title: The New Testament Bible- The Gospel of Luke Chapter 7

Introduction:

Jesus forgives a woman's sin.

Written Verses:

Writing 1-

And he turned to the woman/ and said unto Simon: seeist thou this woman: I entered into thy house/ and thou gavest me no water to my feet: but she hath washed my feet with tears/ and wiped them with the hairs of her head.

Writing 2-

Thou gavest me no kiss: but she/ since the time I came in/ hath not ceased to kiss my feet.

Writing 3-

Mine head with oil thou didest not anoint: and she hath anointed my feet with ointment.

Writing 4-

Wherefore I say unto thee: many sins are forgiven her/ because she loved much

Writing 5-

To whom less is forgiven/ the same doith less love.

Writing 6-

And he said unto her thy sins are forgiven thee.

Written Thought Response Assignment for Module 3 Learning Outcome 15

Directions:

Read both module learning outcome readings. Then provide your own original thoughts based on what you read. Use the suggested guide below to help you gather your thoughts.

- Think about what you liked about both readings.
- Think about what you didn't like about both readings.
- Think about what was interesting to you about both readings.

After thinking about the above suggested guides, write and summarize your final thoughts about both readings in six (6) sentences or less.

Write Your Final Thoughts for Module 3 Learning Outcome 15 In The Space Below:

Sentence 1-

Sentence 2-

Sentence 3-

Sentence 4-

Sentence 5-

Sentence- 6-

Module 3 Vocabulary Assignment

Directions:

Each module you will define three (3) words that are mentioned or relevant to the topics discussed within the module. Use the end of the book to read the author's definition of word that's listed, then search, find, and read the word using a different source such as (book, individual, computer), and then finally write the definition in your own words.

Choose from the following list of words for Module 3:

Individual
Family
Village
Community
Country
World
Sabbath
Society

Word #1:

Author's Definition:

Source Definition:

Your Definition:

Word #2:

Author's Definition:

Source Definition:

Your Definition:

<u>Word #3:</u>

Author's Definition:

Source Definition:

Your Definition:

Chapter 4

Module 4

Module 4

Analyze two strategies to answer the question "Where Am I Going In The Future As A Person Living On Earth?"

Overview of Module 4

This module explores the human and self-discovery. The cry that's heard steers the soul of the human. Begin to seek truth in order to nurture the soul. Life begins and ends with the spirit. Nurture life and seek. Live today and create tomorrow.

When Two Becomes One

Heart to heart love withstands the world's iron rod.

Belief and truth align while holding the hands of God.

Through pain and sorrow growth within one opens love.

Love gives and breathes life into truth sent from above.

Together man and spirit builds from the heart.

What's created gives the world a new start.

When man and spirit become one.

Life is nurtured, created, and won.

By Dawei

The following outcomes will be the focus of this module:

Module 4: Learning Outcome 16- Demonstrate an understanding of the conscious mind.

Module 4: Learning Outcome 17-Demonstrate an understanding of the unconscious mind.

Module 4: Learning Outcome 18-Demonstrate knowledge of positive influences on the mind.

Module 4: Learning Outcome 19- Demonstrate knowledge of negative influences on the mind.

Module 4: Learning Outcome 20- Demonstrate knowledge of the word "Imagination".

Module 4: Learning Outcome 21- Demonstrate knowledge of the word "Belief".

Module 4: Learning Outcome 16

Demonstrate an understanding of the conscious mind.

Overview of Module 4: Learning Outcome 16

In this learning outcome individuals will examine thinking and loving as God. Individuals will gain knowledge of honoring the father (God of Abraham) and the son (Jesus Christ).

Module 4 Learning Outcome 16 Reading #1

Title: Bible- Psalms Chapter 139 Verses 1-6

Introduction:

God knows all the humans' thoughts. The human must think and love as God.

Written Verses:

Verse 1-

For the lead player, a David psalm.

Lord, You searched me and You know,

Verse 2-

It is You Who know when I sit and I rise, You fathom my thoughts from afar.

Verse 3-

My path and my lair You winnow, and with all my ways are familiar.

Verse 4-

For there is no word on my tongue

But that You, O Lord, wholly know it.

Verse 5-

From behind and in front You shaped me,

And You set Your palm upon me.

Verse 6-

Knowledge is too wondrous for me,

High above- l cannot attain it.

Module 4 Learning Outcome 16 Reading #2

Title: The New Testament Bible- The Gospel of John Chapter 5

Introduction:

Jesus (the son) listens to God of Abraham (the father) and honors him. The human must listen and honor the Father, the Son, and the Holy Ghost.

Written Verses:

Writing 1-

Then answered Jesus and said unto them; verely/ verely/ I say unto you: the son can do no thing of himself: but that he seeith the father do.

Writing 2-

For whatsoever he doeth/ that doeth the son also.

Writing 3-

For the father loveth the son/ and showeth him all things/ whatsoever he himself doeth.

Writing 4-

And he will show him greater things then these/ because ye should marvel.

Writing 5-

For likewise as the father raiseth up the dead/ and quickeneth them/ even so the son quickeneth whom he will.

Writing 6-

Neither judgeth the father any man: but hath committed all judgement unto the son/ even as they honor thee the father.

Written Thought Response Assignment for Module 4 Learning Outcome 16

Directions:

Read both module learning outcome readings. Then provide your own original thoughts based on what you read. Use the suggested guide below to help you gather your thoughts.

- Think about what you liked about both readings.
- Think about what you didn't like about both readings.
- Think about what was interesting to you about both readings.

After thinking about the above suggested guides, write and summarize your final thoughts about both readings in six (6) sentences or less.

Write Your Final Thoughts for Module 4 Learning Outcome 16 In The Space Below:

Sentence 1-

Sentence 2-

Sentence 3-

Sentence 4-

Sentence 5-

Sentence- 6-

Module 4: Learning Outcome 17

Demonstrate an understanding of the unconscious mind.

Overview of Module 4: Learning Outcome 17

In this learning outcome individuals will examine understanding God and thoughts. Individuals will gain knowledge of the Kingdom of God.

Module 4 Learning Outcome 17 Reading #1

Title: Bible- Proverbs Chapter 16 Verses 1-6

Introduction:

Thought translated from God helps man find truth in all things.

Written Verses:

Verse 1-

Man's is the ordering of thought, but from the Lord is the tongue's

pronouncing.

Verse 2-

All a man's ways are pure in his eyes, but the Lord takes the spirit's

measure.

Verse 3-

Turn over your deeds to the lord, that your plans may be firm-

founded.

Verse 4-

Each act of the lord has its own end; even the wicked, for an evil

day.

Verse 5-

The Lord's loathing is every haughty man, be sure of it, he will not

go scot-free.

Verse 6-

In faithful kindness a crime is atoned, and in the Lord's fear one swerves from evil.

Module 4 Learning Outcome 17 Reading #2

Title: The New Testament Bible- The Gospel of John Chapter 3

Introduction:

Jesus explains how to see the Kingdom of God.

Written Verses:

Writing 1-

For no man could do such miracles as thou doest/ except God were with him: Jesus answered/ and said unto him: verely verely I say unto thee: except that a man be born a new/ he cannot see the Kingdom of God.

Writing 2-

Nicodemus said unto him: how can a man be born/ when he is old? Can he enter into his mother's body and be born again?

Writing 3-

Jesus answered: verely/ verely I say unto thee: except that a man be born of water/ and of the spirit/ he can not enter into the Kingdom of God. That which is born of the flesh/ is flesh. And that which is born of the spirit/ is spirit.

Writing 4-

Marvel not that I said to thee/ ye must be born a new.

Writing 5-

The wind bloweth where he listeth/ and thou hearest his sound:

but thou canst not tell whence he cometh and whether he goeth.

Writing 6-

So is every man that is born of the spirit.

Written Thought Response Assignment for Module 4 Learning Outcome 17

Directions:

Read both module learning outcome readings. Then provide your own original thoughts based on what you read. Use the suggested guide below to help you gather your thoughts.

- Think about what you liked about both readings.
- Think about what you didn't like about both readings.
- Think about what was interesting to you about both readings.

After thinking about the above suggested guides, write and summarize your final thoughts about both readings in six (6) sentences or less.

Write Your Final Thoughts for Module 4 Learning Outcome 17 In The Space Below:

Sentence 1-

Sentence 2-

Sentence 3-

Sentence 4-

Sentence 5-

Sentence- 6-

Module 4: Learning Outcome 18

Demonstrate knowledge of positive influences on the mind.

Overview of Module 4: Learning Outcome 18

In this learning outcome individuals will examine speaking and thinking good thoughts. Individuals will gain knowledge of how to pray.

Module 4 Learning Outcome 18 Reading #1

Title: Bible- Job Chapter 42 Verses 1-6

Introduction:

Job speaks rightly of God. Job recants and repents to God all knowing, omnipotent, and omnipresent.

Written Verses:

Verse 1-

And Job answered the Lord and he said:

Verse 2-

I know You can do anything, and no devising is beyond You.

Verse 3-

"Who is this obscuring counsel without knowledge?" Therefore I told but did not understand, wonders beyond me that I did not know.

Verse 4-

"Hear, pray, and I will speak. Let me ask you, that you may inform me."

Verse 5-

By the ear's rumor I heard of You, and now my eyes has seen You.

Verse 6-

Therefore do l recant, And l repent in dust and ashes.

Module 4 Learning Outcome 18 Reading #2

Title: The New Testament Bible- The Gospel of Luke Chapter 11

Introduction:

Jesus tells one of his disciples what to say when praying.

Written Verses:

Writing 1-

And it fortuned as he was praying in a certain place; when he ceased/ one of his disciples said unto him: Master teach us to pray as Jhon taught his disciples.

Writing 2-

And he said unto them: When ye pray/ say: Our father which arte in heaven/ hallowed be thy name

Writing 3-

Let thy Kingdom come.

Writing 4-

Thy will/ be fulfilled/ even in earth as it is in heaven.

Writing 5-

Our daily bread give us this day.

Writing 6-

And forgive us our sins: for even we forgive every man that trespaseth us/ and lead us not into temptation/ But deliver us from evil Amen.

Written Thought Response Assignment for Module 4 Learning Outcome 18

Directions:

Read both module learning outcome readings. Then provide your own original thoughts based on what you read. Use the suggested guide below to help you gather your thoughts.

- Think about what you liked about both readings.
- Think about what you didn't like about both readings.
- Think about what was interesting to you about both readings.

After thinking about the above suggested guides, write and summarize your final thoughts about both readings in six (6) sentences or less.

Write Your Final Thoughts for Module 4 Learning Outcome 18 In The Space Below:

Sentence 1-

Sentence 2-

Sentence 3-

Sentence 4-

Sentence 5-

Sentence- 6-

Module 4: Learning Outcome 19

Demonstrate knowledge of negative influences on the mind.

Overview of Module 4: Learning Outcome 19

In this learning outcome individuals will examine trusting, loving, and believing God wholeheartedly. Individuals will gain knowledge of overcoming self-doubt.

Module 4 Learning Outcome 19 Reading #1

Title: Bible- Proverbs Chapter 3 Verses 5-10

Introduction:

King Solomon gives advice to his son. He tells him to trust in the Lord with all your heart.

Written Verses:

Verse 5-

Trust in the Lord with all your heart, and do not lean on your discernment.

Verse 6-

Through all your ways know Him, and He will make your paths straight.

Verse 7-

Do not be wise in your own eyes, fear the Lord and swerve from evil.

Verse 8-

Let it be healing for your flesh and a balm to your bones.

Verse 9-

Honor the Lord more than your wealth and than the first fruits of your crop,

Verse 10-

and your barns will be filled with abundance, your vats will burst

with new wine.

Module 4 Learning Outcome 19 Reading #2

Title: The New Testament Bible- The Gospel of Mark Chapter 14

Introduction:

Jesus knows he's about to die soon. He says to his disciples "The spirit is ready/ but the flesh is weak."

Written Verses:

Writing 1-

And they came into a place named gethsemane/ And he said to his disciples: sit ye here/ while I go apart and pray.

Writing 2-

And he took with him Peter/ James/ and Jhon/ and he began to waxe abasshede and to be in an agony.

Writing 3-

And said unto them: My soul is very heavy even unto the death/ tary here and watch.

Writing 4-

And he went forth a little and fell down on the ground and prayed/ That if it were possible/ the hour might pass from him/ And he said: Abba father/ all things are possible unto thee/ take away this cup from me.

Writing 5-

Nevertheless not that l will/ but that thou wilt be done.

Writing 6-

And he came/ and found them sleeping/ and said to Peter: Simon

sleepest thou? Couldest not thou watch with me one hour? Watch

eye/ and pray/ lest ye enter into temptation/ the spirit is ready/
but the flesh is weak.

Written Thought Response Assignment for Module 4 Learning Outcome 19

Directions:

Read both module learning outcome readings. Then provide your own original thoughts based on what you read. Use the suggested guide below to help you gather your thoughts.

- Think about what you liked about both readings.
- Think about what you didn't like about both readings.
- Think about what was interesting to you about both readings.

After thinking about the above suggested guides, write and summarize your final thoughts about both readings in six (6) sentences or less.

Write Your Final Thoughts for Module 4 Learning Outcome 19 In The Space Below:

Sentence 1-

Sentence 2-

Sentence 3-

Sentence 4-

Sentence 5-

Sentence- 6-

Module 4: Learning Outcome 20

Demonstrate knowledge of the word "Imagination"

Overview of Module 4: Learning Outcome 20

In this learning outcome individuals will examine building a foundation that pleases God. Individuals will gain knowledge of Jesus Christ's foundation that was built on earth and in the Kingdom of Heaven.

Module 4 Learning Outcome 20 Reading #1

Title: Bible- Exodus Chapter 33 Verses 18-23

Introduction:

God tells Moses that no human can see his face and live.

Written Verses:

Verse 18-

eyes and I have known you by name." And he said, "Show me, pray, Your

Verse 19-

glory." And He said, "I shall make all My goodness pass in front of you, and I shall invoke the name of the Lord before you. And I shall grant grace to whom I grant grace and have compassion for whom I have compassion."

Verse 20-

And He said, "You shall not be able to see My face, for no human can see

Verse 21-

Me and live." And the Lord said, "Look, there is a place with Me, and you

Verse 22-

Shall take your stance on the crag. And so, when My glory passes

over, I shall put you in the cleft of the crag and shield you with My

palm until I

Verse 23-

have passed over. And I shall take away My palm and you will see

My back, but My face will not be seen."

Module 4 Learning Outcome 20 Reading #2

Title: The New Testament Bible- Corinthians Chapter 3

Introduction:

Paul speaks about building a foundation that adds to the foundation that Jesus Christ laid.

Written Verses:

Writing 1-

We are Goddis laborers: ye are Goddis hunsbandry/ ye are Goddis building.

Writing 2-

According to the grace of God given unto me/ as a wise builder have I laid the foundation/ another hath built there on: but let every man take hede how he buildeth apon.

Writing 3-

For other foundation can no name lay/ then that which is laid/ which is Jesus Christ.

Writing 4-

If any man build on this foundation/ gold/ silver/ precious stones/ timber/ hay/ or stubble: every man's work shall appear.

Writing 5-

For the day shall declare it/ and it shall be showed in fire/ and the fire shall try every man's work what it is.

Writing 6-

If any man work that he hath built apon bide/ he shall receive a reward.

Written Thought Response Assignment for Module 4 Learning Outcome 20

Directions:

Read both module learning outcome readings. Then provide your own original thoughts based on what you read. Use the suggested guide below to help you gather your thoughts.

- Think about what you liked about both readings.
- Think about what you didn't like about both readings.
- Think about what was interesting to you about both readings.

After thinking about the above suggested guides, write and summarize your final thoughts about both readings in six (6) sentences or less.

Write Your Final Thoughts for Module 4 Learning Outcome 20 In The Space Below:

Sentence 1-

Sentence 2-

Sentence 3-

Sentence 4-

Sentence 5-

Sentence- 6-

Module 4: Learning Outcome 21

Demonstrate knowledge of the word "Belief"

Overview of Module 4: Learning Outcome 21

In this learning outcome individuals will examine God's covenant with Abraham, Isaac, and Jacob. Individuals will gain knowledge of why Jesus Christ is the light of the world.

Module 4 Learning Outcome 21 Reading #1

Title: Bible- Exodus Chapter 6 Verses 2-7

Introduction:

God speaks to Moses and tells him to tell the Israelites that he will

free them from Egypt and be their God because of the covenant

that he made with Abraham, Isaac, and Jacob.

Written Verses:

Verse 2-

And God spoke to Moses and said to him, "I

Verse 3-

am the Lord. And I appeared to Abraham, to Isaac, and to Jacob as

El

Verse 4-

Shaddai, but in My name the lord I was not known to them. And I

also established My covenant with them to give them the land of

Canaan, the

Verse 5-

Land of their sojournings in which they sojourned. And also I

Myself have heard the groaning of the Israelites whom the

Egyptians enslave, and I do

Verse 6-

Remember My covenant. Therefore say to the lsraelites: 'l am the
Lord. l will take you out from under the burdens of Egypt and l will
rescue you from their bondage and l will redeem you with an
outstretched arm and

Verse 7-

with great retributions. And l will take you to me as a people and
l will be your God, and you shall know that l am the Lord your God
Who takes

Module 4 Learning Outcome 21 Reading #2

Title: The New Testament Bible- The Gospel of Jhon Chapter 9

Introduction:

Jesus explains he does the work of him that sent him and that he is the light of the world.

Written Verses:

Writing 1-

And as Jesus passed by/ he saw a man which was blind from his birth/ And his disciples asked him saying: Master who did sin: this man/ or his father and mother/ that he was born blind?

Writing 2-

Jesus answered: Neither this man hath sinned/ nor yet his father and mother: but that the works of God should be showed on him.

Writing 3-

I must work the works of him that sent me/ while it is day. The night cometh/ when no man can work.

Writing 4-

As long as I am in the world/ I am the light of the world.

Writing 5-

As soon as he had thus spoken/ he spat on the ground/ and made clay of the spetle/ and rubbed the clay on the eyes of the blind/ and said unto him: Go wash thee in the pool of Siloe (which by interpretation/ signifieth sent).

Writing 6-

He went his way and washed/ and came again seeing.

Written Thought Response Assignment for Module 4 Learning Outcome 21

Directions:

Read both module learning outcome readings. Then provide your own original thoughts based on what you read. Use the suggested guide below to help you gather your thoughts.

- Think about what you liked about both readings.
- Think about what you didn't like about both readings.
- Think about what was interesting to you about both readings.

After thinking about the above suggested guides, write and summarize your final thoughts about both readings in six (6) sentences or less.

Write Your Final Thoughts for Module 4 Learning Outcome 21 In The Space Below:

Sentence 1-

Sentence 2-

Sentence 3-

Sentence 4-

Sentence 5-

Sentence- 6-

Module 4 Vocabulary Assignment

Directions:

Each module you will define three (3) words that are mentioned or relevant to the topics discussed within the module. Use the end of the book to read the author's definition of word that's listed, then search, find, and read the word using a different source such as (book, individual, computer), and then finally write the definition in your own words.

Choose from the following list of words for Module 4:

Mind
Conscious Mind
Unconscious Mind
Influences
Positive Influences
Negative Influences
Slave
Imagination
Faith
Belief
Kingdom of Heaven
Kingdom of God

<u>Word #1:</u>

Author's Definition:

Source Definition:

Your Definition:

<u>Word #2:</u>

Author's Definition:

Source Definition:

Your Definition:

<u>Word #3:</u>

Author's Definition:

Source Definition:

Your Definition:

The following outcomes will be the focus of this module:

Module 5: Learning Outcome 22- Demonstrate knowledge of a problem in society.

Module 5: Learning Outcome 23-Demonstrate knowledge of how to solve a problem in society.

Module 5: Learning Outcome 24-Demonstrate knowledge how a person can develop themself to help people in the world.

Module 5: Learning Outcome 25- Demonstrate knowledge of how self-development helps solve problems in society.

Module 5: Learning Outcome 26- Demonstrate knowledge of how life is created.

Module 5: Learning Outcome 22

Demonstrate knowledge of a problem in society.

Overview of Module 5: Learning Outcome 22

In this learning outcome individuals will examine what God

hears and sees. Individuals will gain knowledge of being humble.

Module 5 Learning Outcome 22 Reading #1

Title: Bible- Psalm Chapter 94 Verses 5-10

Introduction:

God hears and sees all good and evil that is done. God will judge all things because he made all things on earth.

Written Verses:

Verse 5-

Your people, O Lord, they crush, and Your estate they abuse.

Verse 6-

Widow and sojourner they kill, and orphans they murder.

Verse 7-

And they say, "Yah will not see, and the God of Jacob will not heed."

Verse 8-

Take heed, you brutes in the people, and you fools, when will you be wise?

Verse 9-

Who plants the ear, will He not hear? Who fashions the eye, will He not look?

Verse 10-

The chastiser of nations, will He not punish, Who teaches humankind knowledge?

Module 5 Learning Outcome 22 Reading #2

Title: The New Testament Bible- The Gospel of Luke Chapter 18

Introduction:

Jesus explains that man should not despise others. Every man that goes before God should humble himself and praise the almighty God.

Written Verses:

Writing 1-

And he put forth this similitude/ unto certain which trusted in themselves/ that they were perfect/ and despised others.

Writing 2-

Two men went up into the temple to pray: the one a pharise/ and the other a publican.

Writing 3-

The pharise stood and prayed thus with himself. God l thank thee that l am not as others are/ extortioners/ unjust/ adulteres/ and even as this publican is. l fast twice in the week. l give tithe of all that l possess.

Writing 4-

And the publican stood afar of/ and would not lift up his eyes to heaven/ but smote his breast/ saying: God be merciful to me a sinner.

Writing 5-

I tell you: this man departed home to his house justified more then the other.

Writing 6-

For every man that exalteth himself/ shall be brought low: And he that humbleth himself/ shall be exalted.

Written Thought Response Assignment for Module 5 Learning Outcome 22

Directions:

Read both module learning outcome readings. Then provide your own original thoughts based on what you read. Use the suggested guide below to help you gather your thoughts.

- Think about what you liked about both readings.
- Think about what you didn't like about both readings.
- Think about what was interesting to you about both readings.

After thinking about the above suggested guides, write and summarize your final thoughts about both readings in six (6) sentences or less.

Write Your Final Thoughts for Module 5 Learning Outcome 22 In The Space Below:

Sentence 1-

Sentence 2-

Sentence 3-

Sentence 4-

Sentence 5-

Sentence- 6-

Module 5: Learning Outcome 23

Demonstrate knowledge of how to solve a problem in society.

Overview of Module 5: Learning Outcome 23

In this learning outcome individuals will examine the blessings of God. Individuals will gain knowledge of honoring creation on earth and God.

Module 5 Learning Outcome 23 Reading #1

Title: Bible- Exodus Chapter 31 Verses 3-8

Introduction:

God gives blessings with wisdom, knowledge, and understanding to complete tasks he want completed on earth.

Written Verses:

Verse 3-

have called by name Bezalel son of Uri son of Hur, of the tribe of Judah. And I have filled him with the spirit of God in wisdom and in understanding

Verse 4-

and in knowledge and in every task, to devise plans, to work in gold and in

Verse 5-

Silver and in bronze, and in stonecutting for settings and in wood carving,

Verse 6-

to do every task. And I, look, I have set by him Oholiab son of Ahisamach, of the tribe of Dan, and in the heart o every wise-hearted man I have set

Verse 7-

wisdom, that they make all that l have charged you: the Tent of

Meeting and the Ark of the Covenant and the covering that is upon

it and all the

Verse 8-

furnishings of the Tent, and the table and its furnishings and the

pure lamp

Module 5 Learning Outcome 23 Reading #2

Title: The New Testament Bible- The Gospel of Mark Chapter 12

Introduction:

Jesus explains how to honor what's made and done on earth and to honor God.

Written Verses:

Writing 1-

And they sent unto him a certain of the pharises with Herod's servants/ to take him in his words.

Writing 2-

And as soon as they were come/ they said unto him: Master/ we know that thou arte true/ and carest for no man: for thou considerest not the degree of men/ but teachest the way of God truly: is it lawful to pay tribute to Cesar/ or not: ought we to give/ or ought we not to give;

Writing 3-

He knew their dissimulation/ and said unto them: why tempt ye me: Bring me a penny/ that l may see it.

Writing 4-

And they brought him one.

Writing 5-

And he said unto them: whose is this image and superscription?

And they said unto him/ Cesars.

Writing 6-

And Jesus answered/ and said unto them: Then give to Cesar that

which belongeth to Cesar: And give God that which pertaineth to

God.

Written Thought Response Assignment for Module 5 Learning Outcome 23

Directions:

Read both module learning outcome readings. Then provide your own original thoughts based on what you read. Use the suggested guide below to help you gather your thoughts.

- Think about what you liked about both readings.
- Think about what you didn't like about both readings.
- Think about what was interesting to you about both readings.

After thinking about the above suggested guides, write and summarize your final thoughts about both readings in six (6) sentences or less.

Write Your Final Thoughts for Module 5 Learning Outcome 23 In The Space Below:

Sentence 1-

Sentence 2-

Sentence 3-

Sentence 4-

Sentence 5-

Sentence- 6-

Module 5: Learning Outcome 24

Demonstrate knowledge of how a person can develop themselves to help people in the world.

Overview of Module 5: Learning Outcome 24

In this learning outcome individuals will examine loving yourself and loving others. Individuals will gain knowledge of Jesus Christ's gift to the world.

Module 5 Learning Outcome 24 Reading #1

Title: Bible- Psalms Chapter 41 Verses 1-6

Introduction:

Love the poor as you love yourself. Help the poor and those in need. Your gift is a gift to God.

Written Verses:

Verse 1-

To the lead player. A David psalm.

Verse 2-

Happy who looks to the poor. On the day of evil may the Lord make him safe.

Verse 3-

May the Lord guard him and keep him alive. May he be called happy in the land. And do not deliver him to his enemies' maw.

Verse 4-

May the Lord sustain him on the couch of pain. You transformed his whole bed of illness.

Verse 5-

I said, "Lord, grant me grace, heal me, though I offended You."

Verse 6-

My enemies said evil of me: 'When will he die and his name be lost?"

Module 5 Learning Outcome 24 Reading #2

Title: The New Testament Bible- The Gospel of Mark Chapter 16

Introduction:

Mary Magdalen, Mary Jacobi, and Salome went to anoint Jesus. Jesus rises from death.

Written Verses:

Writing 1-

And when the sabbath day was past/ Mary Magdalen/ and Mary Jacobi/ and Salome/ bought ointments/ that they might come and anoint him.

Writing 2-

And early in the morning the next day after the sabbath day they came unto the sepuclre/ when the sun was risen/ And they said one to another: who shall roll away the stone from the door of the sepulcre? And when they beheld it/ they saw how the stone was rolled away.

Writing 3-

For it was a very great one/ and they went into the sepulcre/ and saw a young man/ sitting on the right side/ clothed in a long white garment/ and they were abasshed.

Writing 4-

He said unto them/ be not afraid/ ye seek Jesus of Nazareth/ which was crucified.

Writing 5-

He is risen/ He is not here. Behold the place/ where they put him.

Writing 6-

But go your way/ and tell his disciples/ and namely Peter/ that he is gone before you into Galile/ there shall ye see him/ as he said unto you.

Written Thought Response Assignment for Module 5 Learning Outcome 24

Directions:

Read both module learning outcome readings. Then provide your own original thoughts based on what you read. Use the suggested guide below to help you gather your thoughts.

- Think about what you liked about both readings.
- Think about what you didn't like about both readings.
- Think about what was interesting to you about both readings.

After thinking about the above suggested guides, write and summarize your final thoughts about both readings in six (6) sentences or less.

Write Your Final Thoughts for Module 5 Learning Outcome 24 In The Space Below:

Sentence 1-

Sentence 2-

Sentence 3-

Sentence 4-

Sentence 5-

Sentence- 6-

Module 5: Learning Outcome 25

Demonstrate knowledge of how a person can develop themselves to help people in the world.

Overview of Module 5: Learning Outcome 25

In this learning outcome individuals will examine giving praise to the Lord God. Individuals will gain knowledge of Jesus Christ's resurrection.

Module 5 Learning Outcome 25 Reading #1

Title:

Bible- Psalms Chapter 117 Verses 1-2

Bible- Psalms Chapter 118 Verses 1-4

Introduction:

Praise the Lord God. Humble yourself to the Lord God.

Written Verses:

Verse 1-

Praise the Lord, all nations; extol Him, all peoples.

Verse 2-

For His kindness overwhelms us, and the Lord's steadfast truth is

forever. Hallelujah.

Verse 1-

Acclaim the Lord, for He is good, forever His kindness.

Verse 2-

Let Israel now say: forever is His kindness.

Verse 3-

Let the house of Aaron now say: forever is His kindness.

Verse 4-

Let those who fear the Lord now say: forever is His kindness.

Module 5 Learning Outcome 25 Reading #2

Title: The New Testament Bible- The Gospel of Mark Chapter 16

Introduction:

Jesus rose from death. Mary Magdalen saw him first.

Written Verses:

Writing 1-

When Jesus was risen the morrow after the sabbath day/ he appeared first to Mary magdalen/ out of whom he cast seven devils.

Writing 2-

And she went/ and told them that were with him/ as they mourned and wept.

Writing 3-

 And when they heard/ that he was alive/ and had appeared to her: they believed it not.

Writing 4-

After that/ he appeared unto two of them in a strange figure/ as they walked/ and went into the country.

Writing 5-

And they went/ and told it to remnaunt. And they believed them neither.

Writing 6-

After that he appeared unto the eleven as they sat at meate: and cast in their teche their unbelief/ and hardness of heart: because they believed not them which had scene him after his resurrection. And he said unto them. Go ye into all the world/ and preach the Gospel to all creatures: whosoever believeth/ and is baptized/ shall be safe: And whosoever believeth not/ shall be dampned.

Written Thought Response Assignment for Module 5 Learning Outcome 25

Directions:

Read both module learning outcome readings. Then provide your own original thoughts based on what you read. Use the suggested guide below to help you gather your thoughts.

- Think about what you liked about both readings.
- Think about what you didn't like about both readings.
- Think about what was interesting to you about both readings.

After thinking about the above suggested guides, write and summarize your final thoughts about both readings in six (6) sentences or less.

Write Your Final Thoughts for Module 5 Learning Outcome 25 In The Space Below:

Sentence 1-

Sentence 2-

Sentence 3-

Sentence 4-

Sentence 5-

Sentence- 6-

Module 5: Learning Outcome 26

Demonstrate knowledge of how life is created.

Overview of Module 5: Learning Outcome 26

In this learning outcome individuals will examine giving praise to the Lord Go. Individuals will gain knowledge of Jesus Christ's resurrection.

Module 5 Learning Outcome 26 Reading #1

Title: Bible- Exodus Chapter 20 Verses 1-8

Introduction:

God speaks to Moses and Aaron on Mount Sinai.

Written Verses:

Verse 1-

And God spoke all these words, saying: "I am

Verse 2-

The Lord your God who brought you out of the land of Egypt, out of the

Verse 3-

House of slaves. You shall have no other gods besides Me. You shall make

Verse 4-

You no carved likeness and no image of what is in the heavens above or

Verse 5-

What is on the earth below or what is in the waters beneath the earth. You shall not bow to them and you shall not worship them, for l am the Lord your God, a jealous god, reckoning the crime of fathers, with sons, with

Verse 6-

The third generation and with the fourth, for My foes, and doing kindness to the thousandth generation for My friends and for those who keep My

Verse 7-

Commands. You shall not take the name of the Lord your God in vain, for

Verse 8-

The Lord will not acquit whosoever takes His name in vain. Remember

Module 5 Learning Outcome 26 Reading #2

Title: Bible- Exodus Chapter 20 Verses 9-17

Introduction:

God tells Moses and Aaron what to say to the priest and all of the Israelites.

Written Verses:

Verse 9-

the sabbath da to hallow it. Six days you shall work and you shall do all

Verse 10-

your tasks, but the seventh day is a sabbath to the Lord your God. You shall do no task, you and your son and your daughter, your male slave and your slavegirl and your beast and your sojourner who is within your gates.

Verse 11-

 For six days did the Lord make the heavens and the earth, the sea and all that is in it, and He rested on the seventh day. Therefore did the Lord bless

Verse 12-

the sabbath day and hallow it. Honor your father and your mother, so that your days may be long on the soil that the Lord your God has given you.

Verse 13-

You shall not murder.

Verse 14-

You shall not commit adultery.

Verse 15-

You shall not steal.

Verse 16-

You shall not bear false witness against your fellow man.

Verse 17-

You shall not covet your fellow man's house. You shall not covet your fellow man's wife, or his male slave, or his slavegirl, or his ox, or his donkey, or anything that your fellow man has."

Written Thought Response Assignment for Module 5 Learning Outcome 26

Directions:

Read both module learning outcome readings. Then provide your own original thoughts based on what you read. Use the suggested guide below to help you gather your thoughts.

- Think about what you liked about both readings.
- Think about what you didn't like about both readings.
- Think about what was interesting to you about both readings.

After thinking about the above suggested guides, write and summarize your final thoughts about both readings in six (6) sentences or less.

Write Your Final Thoughts for Module 5 Learning Outcome 26 In The Space Below:

Sentence 1-

Sentence 2-

Sentence 3-

Sentence 4-

Sentence 5-

Sentence- 6-

Module 5 Vocabulary Assignment

Directions:

Each module you will define three (3) words that are mentioned or relevant to the topics discussed within the module. Use the end of the book to read the author's definition of word that's listed, then search, find, and read the word using a different source such as (book, individual, computer), and then finally write the definition in your own words.

Choose from the following list of words for Module 5:

Good Problem
Bad Problem
Society
Love
Hate

<u>Word #1:</u>

Author's Definition:

Source Definition:

Your Definition:

<u>Word #2:</u>

Author's Definition:

Source Definition:

Your Definition:

Word #3:

Author's Definition:

Source Definition:

Your Definition:

Project

Modules 1-5 Project

Directions:

Use the space below on this page to draw a picture of yourself helping the world.

Project Picture

Project Picture

Project Picture

Project Picture

Project Picture

Post Test

Directions: Answer the twenty- five multiple choice questions. Use the answer key located at the end of the book to check your answers.

Question 1
What image did God of Abraham create the human?

  a. Water
  b. Moon
  c. His Own Image
  d. A Bird
  e. The Soil

Question 2
How many great lights did God create for the earth?

  a. 1
  b. 4
  c. 8
  d. 2
  e. 12

Question 3
How did the virgin Mary conceive Jesus ?

  a. Of the Holy Ghost
  b. Her Husband Joseph
  c. King David
  d. John the Baptist
  e. None of the Above

Question 4

Who did God of Abraham say he was when he spoke to Moses?

a. I Go There
b. I Am
c. I See As Him
d. I Do This Thing
e. I Will Be Who I Will Be

Question 5

Who did Jesus say would rebuke the world of sin when he leaves?

a. That Comforter
b. John the Baptist
c. The Pharise
d. Cesar
e. None of the above

Question 6

What did God make the Human from?

a. The Soil
b. Different Animal Parts
c. A Bird
d. An Ape
e. None of the above

Question 7

What thing beguiled the man and woman to eat from the tree they were commanded not to eat from?

    a. Dog
    b. Serpent
    c. Bird
    d. Cat
    e. Soil

Question 8

What is the sign of the covenant that God made with Noah that God will not create a flood to destroy the earth again?

    a. A Vinyard
    b. A Boat
    c. A Dove
    d. A Bow Set In The Clouds
    e. None of the Above

Question 9

What is the name of Abraham's son that Sarah gave birth to?

    a. Jacob
    b. Abraham
    c. John
    d. Joseph
    e. Isaac

Question 10

What type of treasures did Jesus say to gather?

a. Diamonds
b. Treasures on earth
c. Treasurers to gather in heaven
d. Gold
e. Animals

Question 11

How old was Abram when he left the land of his birthplace?

a. 18
b. 30
c. 50
d. 99
e. 75

Question 12

Jesus explains that being and believing like what is the greatest in Heaven?

a. King
b. Pharise
c. Spirit
d. Child
e. Disciple

Question 13

What did Jesus do for his disciples that he said they should do to others?

    a. Caught Fish
    b. Washed Their Feet
    c. Took Them To Get Baptized
    d. Gave Them Gold
    e. Gave Them Land

Question 14

What day is a Sabbath day for the Lord God?

    a. First
    b. Third
    c. Second
    d. Seventh
    e. Sixth

Question 15

What did Jesus say to his eleven disciples when he saw them after rising from death?

    a. Hello
    b. Goodbye
    c. All power is given unto me in heaven and earth
    d. I have no power
    e. None of the above

Question 16

Who did Joseph forgive when he was in Egypt?

    a. The people of the town
    b. The King
    c. His Father
    d. His Wife
    e. His Brothers

Question 17

Who knows all of the humans' thoughts?

    a. An Animal
    b. God
    c. The Disciples
    d. A Fortune Teller
    e. None of the Above

Question 18

Who does Jesus Christ Honor?

    a. Gold
    b. Silver
    c. Cesar
    d. The Father
    e. Animals

Question 19

When saying "The Lord's Prayer", what should be fulfilled on earth as it is in Heaven?

a. Greed
b. Happiness
c. Hate
d. Wealth and Power
e. God's Will

Question 20

What advice did King Solomon give to his son?

a. Gain all power in the land
b. Gather gold, silver, and oil
c. Trust in the Lord with all your heart
d. Own as many animals as you can
e. None of the above

Question 21

What does God tell Moses about any human that sees his face?

a. They will be happy
b. They will fly like a bird
c. They will swim like a fish
d. They will not see his face and live
e. They will become wealthy

Question 22

What foundation did Paul speak about adding to?

    a. A house
    b. Cesar
    c. John the Baptists
    d. Peter
    e. Jesus Christ

Question 23

Why did God free the Israelites from Egypt?

    a. Because of the covenant he made with Abraham, Isaac, and Jacob
    b. Because of the King of Egypt
    c. Because there was no one to work the land
    d. Because of Moses
    e. Because of the covenant he made with the King of Egypt.

Question 24

What does Jesus say he is as long as he is in the world?

    a. The star of the world
    b. The wealthiest of the world
    c. The dark of the world
    d. The light of the world
    e. The poorest of the world

Question 25

What does Jesus say that every man should do that goes before God?

a. Sing
b. Cry
c. Give him gold, land, and oil
d. Humble themselves and give praise
e. Run and hide

Chapter 6

Bonus

The Lord's Prayer

Jesus Christ tells one of his disciples what to say when praying.

And he said unto them: When ye pray/ say:

Our father which arte in heaven/ hallowed be thy name

Let thy Kingdom come.

Thy will/ be fulfilled/ even in earth as it is in heaven.

Our daily bread give us this day.

And forgive us our sins: for even we forgive every man that

trespaseth us/ and lead us not into temptation/ But deliver us

from evil Amen.

Chapter 7

Glossary

Note: Below is the author's definition of some of the words used throughout this book.

Air- God of Abrahams breath of love to the human. The breath of life. A life sustaining source created by God of Abraham that is unseen.

Bad Problem- A negative situation, event, cause, happening, or thing that temporarily exists.

Belief- Devotion and commitment to a way of life, spirituality, or religious following.

Conscious Mind- the area of an individual's mind where awareness by the individual of what was seen or happened to the individual is known. The conscious mind gives what is known to the unconscious mind through the human senses. The unconscious mind then remembers and stores what was given by the conscious mind through the human senses.

Community- a group of individuals who live in an area within a country that share similar experiences, beliefs, faith, and way of life.

Country- a group of individuals who live in a specific area of the world that identify with and follow the guidelines set forth by a government or ruling authority required to live a certain way of life in that specific area of the world.

Day- An atmosphere for earth created by God of Abraham. The Sun gives light to the day.

Earth- A formed body of energy consisting of water, air, and soil in the universe created by God of Abraham.

Emotions- A state of influence that is created and nurtured by interaction with an environment, a human, a thing, or mental awareness of something seen or unseen.

Energy- An adaptable source created by God of Abraham that can be seen or unseen.

Family- a group of individuals who live in an area within a village that share similar experiences, beliefs, faith, and way of life. The group of individuals that make up a family may also share more common ancestry than what is found in a village, community, or country.

Faith- An understanding and belief in a way of life, spirituality, or religious following.

God of Abraham- The God of all gods. The God that created heaven, earth, and all things seen and unseen.

Good Problem- A positive situation, event, cause, happening, or thing that temporarily exists.

Hate- A bad emotional state within the body of a human or a thing that influences the mind and will of a being or thing.

Heaven- The place where Jesus Christ is sitting at the right hand of God. Jesus Christ is the way to Heaven. Jesus Christ is the way to the Father. The Holy Spirit is the way to Jesus Christ.

Holy Ghost- The living source of God of Abraham and all things seen and unseen. The Father of Jesus Christ. Jesus Christ was born from the virgin Mary by the Holy Ghost. Jesus Christ was born without sin.

Holy Spirit- The living source of God of Abraham, Jesus Christ, the Holy Ghost, and all things seen and unseen. The gift from Jesus Christ to the world. Except for Jesus Christ, all of mankind was born in sin because of Adam's sin in the garden of Eden. Jesus Christ, who was born without sin, died for all of mankind's sin and gave the Holy Spirit back to the human.

Human- The physical and spirit being created by the God of Abraham in his image to inhabit the planet earth.

Human Senses- Natural intelligences created by the God of Abraham for the human. They include hearing, smelling, touching, speaking, seeing, intuition, and all other natural intelligences that are created by God of Abraham.

Imagination- A vision, image, or thought that originates in the mind.

Individual- A human living on earth.

Jesus Christ- The son of God of Abraham.

Kingdom of Heaven- The established kingdom created and ruled by the God of Abraham for the God of Abraham. Jesus Christ, the Son of God has all power and authority granted to him in the Kingdom of Heaven. Jesus Christ is King. Jesus Christ is the way to the Kingdom of Heaven. Jesus Christ is the way to the Father. The Holy Spirit is the way to Jesus Christ.

Kingdom of God- God of Abraham's established kingdom on earth that resembles the Kingdom of Heaven. God's Will done on earth. Jesus Christ, the Son of Man has all power and authority granted to him in the Kingdom of God. Jesus Christ is King. The Gospel that Jesus Christ taught. Jesus Christ is the way to the Kingdom of God. Jesus Christ is the way to the Father. The Holy Spirit is the way to Jesus Christ.

Love- A good emotional state within the body of a human or a thing that influences the mind and will of a being or thing.

Living- The physical and spirit presence of breath, life, water, and energy in a human, animal, or thing.

Mind- The seen and unseen areas of the human brain that receives and forms thoughts. The mind is made up of both the conscious and unconscious mind and the seen (parts of the brain that can be seen) and unseen (parts of the brain that can't be seen).

Negative Influences- Individuals, energy, situations, physical locations, actions, or any other thing that cause bad problems to occur.

Night- An atmosphere for earth created by God of Abraham. The Moon gives light to the night.

Planet- A formed body of energy in the universe created by God of Abraham.

Positive Influences- Individuals, energy, situations, physical locations, actions, or any other thing that cause good problems to occur.

Sabbath- A holy day for God of Abraham. No task of any kind shall be done on this day. God created the earth, humans, and all things in six days and rested on the seventh day.

Slave- A slave is a living human, animal, or thing on earth that has their body, mind, will, emotions, income, or time controlled by another living human or thing on earth.

Society- a group of individuals who may live within a family, village, community, country, or the world that share similar experiences, beliefs, faith, and way of life.

Spirituality- The examination, study, or belief of God. A way to understand God and the spirit nature of things seen or unseen.

Unconscious Mind- the area of an individual's mind where awareness by the individual of what was seen or happened to the individual is unknown. The unconscious mind remembers and stores what was seen or happened through the human senses.

Village- a group of individuals who live in an area within a community that share similar experiences, beliefs, faith, and way of life.

Water- A life sustaining source created by God of Abraham that is seen.

World- All humans, animals, plants, and all other living things that are living on the planet earth. All living things on earth was created by the God of Abraham. The human was created in God's image. All things seen and unseen was created by God of Abraham.

Chapter 8

Answer Key

Pre-Test Answer Key

1. C

2. D

3. A

4. E

5. A

6. A

7. B

8. D

9. E

10. C

11. E

12. D

13. B

14. D

15. C

16. E

17. B

18. D

19. E

20. C

21. D

22. E

23. A

24. D

25. D

Post Test Answer Key

1. C

2. D

3. A

4. E

5. A

6. A

7. B

8. D

9. E

10. C

11. E

12. D

13. B

14. D

15. C

16. E

17. B

18. D

19. E

20. C

21. D

22. E

23. A

24. D

25. D

Write Your Final Thoughts Below

Write Your Final Thoughts Below

www.ingramcontent.com/pod-product-compliance
Lightning Source LLC
Chambersburg PA
CBHW020433130626
46549CB00001B/115